Accelerating Revenue

Your Definitive Guide to the Theory and Practice of Go-to-Market Enablement

Roz Greenfield and Amanda Leikam
Founders of Level213

Copyright © 2024 by Roz Greenfield and Amanda Leikam

All rights reserved. No portion of this book may be reproduced in any form without written permission from the authors/publishers, except as permitted by U.S. copyright law.

ISBN 9798346298458
Library of Congress Number 2024924224

Book cover, layout and illustrations by Rusty Howson

First edition 2024

Published by Roz Greenfield and Amanda Leikam
San Francisco, CA

For permissions and all other inquiries, visit: level213.com

Contents

Preface   5
Introduction   7

PART ONE: Foundations   11

An Overview of Enablement

    Chapter 1: What Is GTM Enablement?   13
    Chapter 2: Impact to the Organization   17
    Chapter 3: Your First 90 Days in Enablement   25
    Chapter 4: Objectives and Metrics   29

Leveraging Instructional Design

    Chapter 5: Teaching Adults, Training Professionals   33
    Chapter 6: Instructional Design Fundamentals   39
    Chapter 7: Designing Learning Objectives   47
    Chapter 8: Assessing Outcomes   53

Building & Delivering Content

    Chapter 9: Subject Matter Experts, Knowledge Engineering, and Course Facilitation   61
    Chapter 10: Designing and Delivering a Complete Program   71

PART TWO: A Closer Look at Enablement Projects — 77

Typical Projects and Programs

- **Chapter 11:** GTM New Hire Onboarding — 79
- **Chapter 12:** 30/60/90-Day Plans for GTM New Hire Onboarding — 89
- **Chapter 13:** Sales/Success Process — 101
- **Chapter 14:** Product Training and Resources — 109
- **Chapter 15:** Competitive Intelligence and Deep Dives — 115
- **Chapter 16:** Revenue Generating Skills — 119
- **Chapter 17:** Coaching and Mentoring — 123
- **Chapter 18:** GTM Kickoff, Midyear Kickoff, and Quarterly Business Reviews — 135
- **Chapter 19:** Resource Development — 149
- **Chapter 20:** Technology Systems and Tools — 157

Reference Guide: Resources and Glossary — 161
Citations — 165
Acknowledgments — 169
About the Authors — 171

Preface

Welcome to *Accelerating Revenue*, Level213's definitive guide to the theory and practice of go-to-market enablement.

Level213 is a Silicon Valley–based boutique revenue enablement consultancy, founded to solve the challenges faced by growing companies. We've worked in sales, sales management, revenue enablement, consulting, training, and coaching within companies of all stages, from newly funded startups to global enterprises. Our expertise is with hyper-growth companies, enabling all pre- and post-sale go-to-market (GTM) roles, as well as managers throughout the organization. We've consistently noticed that these companies have innovative products/services and aggressive revenue goals but lack the infrastructure, strategy, and skill set to achieve them. They may recognize the importance of enablement, training, and coaching, but they don't have these critical resources built into their organizations. This lack is why we launched our firm, and why we've been so successful.

Before we go further, let's answer your first question… Why did we name our company Level213, and how do you pronounce it? We're Level "two-thirteen" because we are change agents. Water changes state at 212 degrees Fahrenheit, but why stop there? We believe the threshold of change is only the beginning; we want to take you further, to level up to the next degree.

One of the most rewarding aspects of our work has been building out and delivering best-in-class training programs that support GTM revenue enablement professionals. In other words, we enable Enablement. We designed our programs to serve the growing population of people tasked with enablement responsibilities but lacking the guidance and mentorship necessary to effectively support the GTM teams within their companies.

We've developed and refined our methods over years of working 1:1 with enablement professionals who were new to enablement roles. As part of our Apprenticeship program, they mastered the theoretical understanding and strategic capabilities essential to establishing successful GTM Revenue Enablement functions. Our program has been tremendously successful, with many of our early graduates now leading their own teams and serving in strategic enablement leadership roles.

Our success lies in constantly challenging ourselves to best support enablement professionals in a growing and ever-evolving space. This guidebook is one of those efforts. We've adapted the content from the programs mentioned above and present it here in book form for you to consume at your own pace. Our hope is that these lessons allow you to build the informed foundation you need to run an effective enablement function at your company, and that they point you toward additional learning opportunities you may wish to pursue to meet your individual goals. We're thrilled to make our expertise available to an enablement audience beyond our direct clients, and we're honored to support you in your enablement career.

Introduction

This book is intended to support GTM enablement professionals with the core information needed to succeed in a modern enablement role. Many successful businesses today rely on an enablement function as a proven revenue multiplier that sits between the Sales, Success, Product, Marketing, and Operations teams. Often, however, there isn't the necessary expertise within the company to effectively mentor and develop the enablement professionals who are critical to the company's continued growth. Providing this expertise, bridging this gap, and "enabling Enablement" is a big part of why we created our consultancy.

Our focus has been Software as a Service (SaaS) technology companies, but the concepts and approaches we present can be applied within any industry. The underlying premise of all enablement is empowering customer-facing reps and management with the communication skills, processes, tools, and strategies that optimize engagement and produce revenue.

We offer the information in this book with the assumption that, regardless of industry, you are established in an enablement role, are newly promoted into the role, are looking to grow your skill set to position yourself for the jump into enablement, or are someone who needs enablement insights. Perhaps you don't have a formal enablement role (e.g., you are a Sales leader or cross-functional stakeholder such as Revenue

Operations or Product Marketing) but have been tasked with providing resources to move the needle on your team's productivity and need a more comprehensive understanding of how you can effectively support and partner with the Enablement function.

We're also assuming that you are familiar with the general operations, structures, and roles within a revenue generating organization. No matter your tenure, the guidelines, recommendations, best practices, and tools we present are intended as key reference points for the current projects you will be working on, as well as a long-term resource you can turn to throughout your enablement career. We use the term "sales" to encompass any role in the sales cycle leading up to a closed deal. We use the term "success" to refer to any role in the post-sale and customer management/retention cycle. When not referring to a specific role, we will often use the term "rep" to refer to any customer-facing representative, team member, or employee in a GTM role. For any terms or acronyms that need clarification, please refer to the Glossary at the end of the book.

At the end of each chapter, you'll find a Debrief and Applied Learning section. Debrief questions are designed to help you reflect on how each chapter's ideas may or may not be at play in your organization. Applied Learning prompts are intended to help you proactively engage with the ideas presented in the context of your current work environment. Many chapters also conclude with suggestions for related episodes from our podcast, *Fueling the Revenue Engine*, or our blog, *Next Level Thoughts*. Both of these resources can be found at level213.com.

When approaching the content in this book, our recommendation is to complete the chapters sequentially in Part One, then proceed to the chapters in Part Two in the order that's most relevant to you at this time. Part Two is a reference that you can return to again and again throughout your enablement career, as your priorities and responsibilities expand. To give you a better idea of how the topics build, we've organized them as follows.

PART ONE: Foundations

An Overview of Enablement: Chapters 1–4

This book will be most helpful to you if we work from a shared understanding of how GTM enablement works. We start with a holistic review of the Enablement function, a look at how it impacts the GTM organization, an outline of the first 90 days in an enablement role, and a discussion of key objectives and metrics.

Leveraging Instructional Design: Chapters 5–8

This section introduces the science of adult learning and how successful GTM enablement programs build on instructional design principles. We'll cover how to define learning objectives and assess outcomes, noting the importance of Bloom's Taxonomy as a framework to guide your designs. Without a command of these topics, training programs almost invariably fall short.

Building & Delivering Content: Chapters 9–10

Grounded in the foundations of GTM enablement and adult learning theory, you're now ready to put it all together. Here we cover working with subject matter experts, knowledge engineering, course facilitation, and how to ensure that all phases of your programs are successful, from design to delivery.

PART TWO: A Closer Look at Enablement Projects

Typical Projects and Programs: Chapters 11–20

Having covered the essentials of successful GTM enablement, we now present a range of additional projects that typically fall to the Enablement team. Some of these topics will be of more immediate interest to you, and we invite you to start with the chapters most relevant to your current needs and priorities. For the topics that aren't immediately relevant, we suggest that you review them for a high-level understanding of various scenarios that you're likely to face at some point in your enablement career and then refer back to those chapters in more detail when needed.

Please note that all of the tables, templates, and additional resources you'll find in this book are available for download at level213.com.

PART ONE: Foundations

In Part One, we'll cover the foundations of enablement, offering reflections on how and why enablement came to be, where it typically sits now in relation to GTM teams, and how to strategize for success in your enablement career. We'll also delve into instructional design, explaining how to plan and deliver highly effective and impactful programs for the teams you support—and why the methods we endorse work.

We'll unpack the details in the following chapters:
An Overview of Enablement
    Chapter 1: What Is GTM Enablement?
    Chapter 2: Impact to the Organization
    Chapter 3: Your First 90 Days in Enablement
    Chapter 4: Objectives and Metrics
Leveraging Instructional Design
    Chapter 5: Teaching Adults, Training Professionals
    Chapter 6: Instructional Design Fundamentals
    Chapter 7: Designing Learning Objectives
    Chapter 8. Assessing Outcomes
Building & Delivering Content
    Chapter 9: Subject Matter Experts, Knowledge Engineering, and Course Facilitation
    Chapter 10: Designing and Delivering a Complete Program

Whether you're coming from a sales, account management, training, education, or perhaps human resources background, these topics are essential to your success in any enablement endeavor. We encourage you to leverage this information as you build your expertise and hone your execution. If, as you explore these ideas, you'd like additional support putting them into practice, you can reach us at level213.com/contact.

Chapter 1:
What Is GTM Enablement?

The foundation of GTM enablement, also known as revenue enablement or sales enablement, is to provide direct, customer-facing roles with the programs, knowledge, and resources they need to successfully engage buyers and customers throughout the customer journey and ultimately increase revenue.

> **Definition:** GTM enablement ensures that customer-facing professionals engage customers at the right time and place with optimal competencies—and appropriate insights, messages, content, and assets—to provide value and ease throughout the customer's journey.

GTM enablement optimizes the selling motion and supporting processes in the buying experience by using the right revenue and performance management technologies and practices, while leveraging relevant cross-functional capabilities. GTM enablement increases pipeline, moves opportunities forward, wins deals more effectively, expands and grows accounts, and drives profitable growth.

Enablement professionals are somewhat akin to museum curators. A curator creates an exhibit from artists or history, weaving the story arc and context so that the public can experience and enjoy it. Similarly, an enablement professional creates and curates the knowledge and resources that the Sales and Success teams need, presenting them in a way that can be accessed and leveraged during real-time customer communications.

GTM enablement works to:
- Eliminate roadblocks so customer-facing sales and success teams can focus on bringing in new and/or expanded business
- Align processes and goals across the sales, marketing, success, and even partnership teams where applicable
- Ensure that reps get the tools, content, training, and coaching they need to maximize their ability to achieve quota

How does enablement work?

Enablement's responsibilities are multifaceted and often include strategy development, content creation, and training design and delivery, as well as cross-functional collaboration. When working collaboratively, Enablement partners with roles such as revenue leaders and front-line managers (FLMs), Product Marketing, Product, Revenue Operations, and other departments based on GTM needs.

Many companies today offer enablement for multiple groups of customer-facing roles. Depending on the company, they may refer to this collective group as the Revenue Team, Growth Team, Go-to-Market, or simply GTM. Regardless of what it's called, the roles on the team provide coverage for the entire customer journey, from leads being sourced and developed all the way through to longtime customers. For the purposes of this guide, we will refer to enablement for all of these roles as GTM enablement.

As technology evolves and new products and services are created, growing companies have the potential to impact the world in substantial ways. As these businesses scale, their processes, systems, programs, and infrastructure will either support or hinder growth. This uncertainty places revenue leaders in a bind as they try to bridge the gap between their current resources and the goals they are committed to reaching.

At some point, leaders must decide how they want to develop the infrastructure required for growth. GTM Enablement at a company is usually established with a limited scope and then expands through the following three phases of maturity as the company grows:

1. **Reactionary**
   - No formal Enablement team or function
   - Individuals performing enablement duties on an ad-hoc basis
   - No defined onboarding or continued training process
   - Minimal customer-facing assets
   - Content scattered across multiple repositories
   - No documented sales process or customer journey

2. **Project-Based**
   - Cooperation between sales, success, marketing, ops, and enablement teams
   - Defined onboarding and continued training programs
   - Basic tools, technology, and systems to aid productivity
   - Sales assets supporting buyer journey easily accessible
   - Playbook and sales/success process defined

3. **Integrated**
   - Aligned goals across Sales, Success, Marketing, Ops, and Enablement
   - Dynamic and scalable sales and success processes
   - Performance management, coaching, and mentoring programs
   - Role-specific development and training programs for reps and managers
   - Focus on efficiency and scalability of all processes, programs, and systems
   - KPIs clearly defined, tracked, and reported
   - Feedback and data-driven decisions with commitment to continual improvement

Related *Fueling the Revenue Engine* Podcast Episodes:
- Episode 1: Why, What and How of Enablement
- Episode 17: The Intersection of Revenue Operations and Enablement

Chapter 1 Debrief:
- Which enablement maturity phase is your company at today?
- How is the phase impacting the company positively or negatively?
- Where do you want your company's Enablement function to be in the next 12 months?

Applied Learning:
- Moving toward your desired phase of enablement maturity
  - Based on your current enablement maturity phase, sketch out an initial assessment of the challenges and gaps preventing you from reaching the next phase.
  - Create a proposed plan that includes prioritized initiatives that will start bridging the gaps you have identified.

Chapter 2:
Impact to the Organization

The Case for GTM Enablement

In order to be competitive, a successful organization needs a GTM enablement strategy. Companies with best-in-class GTM enablement strategies experience increases in deal size, higher conversion rates, lower customer churn rates, longer tenure for team members, and a larger percentage of their revenue team achieving quota. If a company is not focusing on GTM enablement, there's a good chance competitors in its space are, which allows them to more effectively pursue market share and recruit top talent to their team. For your company to remain a strong player in your industry, consider the following best practices.

Strong GTM Enablement:
- Partners with the GTM teams to build out the insight, tools, and information needed to ultimately increase revenue.
- Partners with Sales/Success management to strike a balance between managing the business, their teams, and ongoing development, while also enabling them to actively reinforce the processes and training programs that have been rolled out.
- Provides Sales and Success team members with the programs, knowledge, and resources they need to

successfully engage the buyer throughout the buying process and customer journey.
- Acts as productivity multipliers and produces the return on GTM headcount investment.

To reap the benefits of an impactful, best-in-class enablement program, the revenue leadership team, the individuals being enabled, and the Enablement team members must be fully committed. The reality is the Enablement team is far smaller than the number of individuals it supports and must serve in a one-to-many capacity. In relative terms, the FLM in particular has day-to-day leadership responsibilities for far fewer individuals and should be enrolled as your partner to leverage and reinforce the enablement programs that support the success and development of their direct teams.

Let's look at the different areas that GTM enablement impacts within the larger revenue organization.

Productivity

Productivity is a major challenge for every organization. There are only so many hours in a day to drive revenue, and yet there are non-revenue generating activities that are constantly competing for time. Even though many revenue leaders acknowledge this, their focus is not on quantifying the economics of lost productivity.

In our work, we've seen the following trends:
- 30% of a rep's week is spent searching for and sharing content relevant to buyers (case studies, product information, etc.).
- Most companies store sales and success related information and resources in up to five or six different repositories.
- 70% of reps say that lack of knowledge is the reason they couldn't close deals or support customers.
- 40% of GTM knowledge is out of date and inaccurate.

The reality is that reps will always have to spend time on activities beyond direct, customer-facing engagement. They are responsible for research, prep, internal team meetings, training, logging notes, and more. But when they need to search for content, get questions answered, and navigate

Figure 2.1: Simple math to illustrate sales productivity losses

Number of reps	50
Hours that each rep loses every week looking for content	7
Average working hours per year for one rep (less PTO)	2,000
Total hours lost per year, per rep	350
Average national base salary per rep	$100,000
Total equivalent productivity dollars lost across team of 50 reps	$875,000

through a buyer journey process that hasn't been optimized or standardized, their productivity is hindered.

A key responsibility of Enablement is to create systems and processes that reduce the roadblocks to productivity and maximize the direct selling/customer-facing time for each rep on a daily basis. The research firm CSO Insights reports increasing selling time as a top enablement priority, second only to decreasing new ramp-up time (CSO Insights, 2016). To understand the importance of preventing productivity losses, which allows for increased selling time, consider the hypothetical scenario below.

To put this into another frame, the $875,000 cost of the productivity hours lost is equivalent to the spend required to pay eight new salespeople for an entire year. Instead of having eight additional sellers, the example company here is accepting a massive productivity loss from their existing team. We don't know of any revenue leader, or CFO for that matter, who wouldn't be alarmed by this loss and wouldn't immediately want to put measures in place to reduce it.

Revenue Effectiveness

If productivity means reps can spend more time selling and supporting customers, revenue effectiveness means reps can generate more revenue during the times they are engaged with prospects and customers. Given equal time, top performers are simply more effective than the average reps on a team. *Enablement programs create more top performers by defining and building repeatable processes that help all reps perform at a higher level.*

In order to improve revenue effectiveness, reps need to understand the mechanics of selling more effectively, as well as the potential pitfalls and things that derail them. In our experience, inability to articulate value is a key hurdle that Enablement needs to help Sales overcome. The importance of facilitating a clearer explanation of why your company's product/service is valuable was the key takeaway from the research firm SiriusDecision's (since acquired by Forrester) 2015 Sales and Marketing Summit. As T. Melissa Madian reported from the summit: "71 percent of sales leaders say it is the salesperson's inability to articulate value to the customer that separates high performers from low performers. Which means only 29 percent of sales conversations hold any value to a customer" (Madian, 2015). In the decade since these statistics highlighted this alarmingly common failure, there has been a groundswell around articulating value, but we have observed only a select minority of companies successfully enabling their reps to actually do so.

A strong GTM enablement program can address the challenge of revenue effectiveness by providing the context, tools, and resources required for reps to consistently build a value proposition that resonates with prospects and customers. This investment of resources extends past the initial sale; it is the foundation of retaining customers and maximizing their lifetime value.

Revenue effectiveness programs typically include:
- Standardized sales methodology, built either in house or through a third party
- A defined buying process and motion mapped to a sales process
- Sales/Success playbooks that include how to position, qualify, and sell throughout the buyer's journey; business drivers; and navigating internal processes
- Skills training and reinforcement coaching to ensure that reps have ongoing competencies in key areas such as positioning, qualifying, articulating value, and differentiation

GTM Onboarding and Training

When done well, GTM onboarding has a huge multiplier effect and a direct line to increased revenue. When the GTM onboarding program is poorly executed, the result can be devastating, dominoing across the company as forecasted revenue based on headcount does not show up on schedule and budgets are impacted in real time. A 2023 study by the sales research firm Bridge Group reinforces this point regarding budget, highlighting a decrease in ramp-up time for new salespeople as a crucial goal (Bridge Group, 2023). Similarly, G2 Learning Hub statistics indicate that 44.9% of organizations prioritize decreasing new salesperson ramp-up time to full productivity as their top sales enablement goal (G2, 2024).

Note: We will cover in depth on how to build and maintain a successful GTM onboarding program in Chapter 11. In this chapter, we're looking at the value an onboarding program brings to an organization as one of the key responsibilities of the Enablement function.

Roughly speaking, the average sales rep in the US represents an investment of $100,000 per year. Many companies, especially in Silicon Valley, pay much more. Faced with the need to deliver on increasing revenue goals and make a return on GTM headcount investments, revenue leaders are keenly aware of the need for training and onboarding programs that help new hires ramp quickly into productivity and effectiveness.

It should be noted that a quick ramp into productivity does not mean an onboarding that is a one-and-done program. Most GTM onboarding programs include an introduction to the company and its culture, processes, and tools, as well as product training. Additional emphasis is placed on the playbook, practice sessions for different buyer personas, and negotiation training across all pricing tiers. Depending on the sophistication and resources of the company, many will adopt differentiated learning through classroom (live or live virtual), self paced, technology hosted, microlearning, peer coaching, etc. Additional coaching and role-plays are also essential elements. The key is for *learning to be supported over time, not just in the first few weeks after a new hire's start date.*

The example below, drawn from numbers we encounter in our work, shows how GTM enablement with an onboarding program impacts revenue contribution, rep tenure, and return on investment for each new sales hire. Put in this context, the value of the training investment is easy to see.

Figure 2.2: Return on training investment

Annual sales rep compensation is $100,000, with an annual quota of $500,000	Scenario A: Minimal training and rep shadowing	Scenario B: 30-day training with monthly reinforcement
Projected sales rep tenure (in months)	12	36
Total sales rep compensation over projected tenure	$100,000	$300,000
Time to first dollar (in months)	3	2
Quota achievement	65%	85%
Revenue sold over sales rep's tenure	$325,000	$1,275,000
ROI	$225,000	$975,000

Sales and Marketing Alignment

Studies have shown that close collaboration between Sales/Success (covering pre- and post-sale) and Marketing can lead to significant improvements in revenue. Conversely, a disconnect between Sales/Success and Marketing can dramatically reduce revenue as well as create massive operating inefficiencies.

GTM Enablement bridges the gap between Sales/Success and Marketing. A dedicated enablement program can close the feedback loop between the departments, inform relevant positioning and content development, improve visibility into content usage, and unify the goals of all teams. As a result, each team will be more productive as it focuses on what it does best. G2 Learning Hub research suggests that Sales and Marketing alignment can help companies become 67% better at closing deals (G2, 2024). Furthermore, technology companies such as Hubspot report that Sales and Marketing misalignment costs businesses $1 trillion each year in decreased sales productivity and wasted marketing efforts (Hubspot, 2017).

When Sales, Success, Marketing, and even Product teams can communicate and collaborate effectively—using the same definition of the customer journey process, as well as an aligned understanding of the selling and retention processes—organizations run much more efficiently. Optimal alignment even filters down to such basic but instrumental details as shared top-of-the-funnel stage definitions (MQL, SQL, Opportunity, etc.) between the teams. As a best practice, we advise Enablement to partner with Marketing to create customer-facing resources for the revenue team—first call decks, case studies, pricing proposal decks, competitive intel, informational pieces for customer events, etc.—that draw from and reinforce the messaging created by Marketing. Enablement should also coordinate with Marketing on all product trainings and buyer persona intel, as well as brand/value messaging by product, persona, and vertical. By sharing resources and staying in close communication, all teams contribute to more wins for the organization.

Related *Fueling the Revenue Engine* Podcast Episodes:
- Episode 2: True Partnership Between Sale Leadership and Enablement
- Episode 9: Strong Sales Enablement and Product Marketing Partnership

Chapter 2 Debrief:
- What are the biggest revenue productivity challenges faced at your company?
- What are the biggest revenue effectivity challenges faced at your company?
- Where do you think the biggest training opportunities lie?
- What are the Sales/Success/Marketing alignment challenges you see?

Applied Learning:
- Think through your current priorities and the requests from across the revenue organization. Which GTM enablement programs do you think are most important to implement first and why?
- Based on your priorities, create an inventory of potential resources needed by the customer-facing reps. Sketch out a timeline for development and rollout of priority resources. It's best practice to meet with Marketing to determine if there are existing assets that can be repurposed or further developed into enablement resources.
- Prepare for and conduct a meeting with the front-line managers to gain their support for a GTM enablement program you are rolling out.
    - Consider the benefits the program will have on their direct reports, the time commitment for them and their teams, and how to best communicate to support each other as partners throughout this program.
- Alternatively, if you are not leading the initiatives, consider:
    - Based on the projects you are working on, where do you think the biggest opportunity is for you to build collaborative relationships with other teams?
    - How could you enroll them with a win-win for both of your teams?

Chapter 3:
Your First 90 Days in Enablement

Depending on the stage of your company's growth, your manager may or may not have clearly defined how to be successful in your role. If your company's Enablement function is brand new, you may very well be co-creating the parameters of this role with your leadership. If you are joining an established Enablement team, understanding how the GTM Enablement function serves the broader organization is nonetheless a critical foundation as you complete your general company onboarding, role-based onboarding and begin your work.

To help you get situated in your new position, we suggest identifying actionable items that can be completed within your first three months.

The suggested activities below have been designed to give you context and help you engage with stakeholders as you start to create your own priorities and programs. Read through the suggestions and select the items that are most applicable to your organization.

- Talk to as many salespeople, customer success managers, sales engineers, members of any other team that you support, and front-line managers as you can to understand what's really going on.
  - Ask as many questions as you can about what's working well, what's challenging or frustrating, where the gaps are, etc. Get curious!
- Listen to real calls with customers and prospects to hear firsthand what is actually being said. You can attend calls live or review calls in a call coaching tool like Gong or Chorus if your team uses such a technology.
  - Even if you've previously been in a selling or customer-facing role, listening from the perspective of Enablement is different. Notice what the rep is missing, what could help them, where their process is effective, and where it's not.
  - Keep in mind your goal is to determine what the team needs in order to improve productivity and effectiveness, not to turn them into clones of you.
- Interview top performers to find out why they are so successful in producing revenue.
  - What are they doing differently to create these results? How did they learn to do this? Think about how you can create a process or resources based on what they are doing that will benefit the entire team.
- Participate in win/loss deal reviews to understand how and why deals are won or lost.
- Meet with GTM leadership to understand your organization's top priorities and goals.
  - Be sure to ask about why these priorities bubbled to the top of the list and what the associated risks are if the initiatives to support them are not successful.
- Meet with subject matter experts (SMEs) like Product Managers and Marketing to understand things like content strategies and product release calendars.
- Attend GTM weekly team meetings to understand the dynamics of the different groups and their leaders.
- Meet with Revenue Operations (or Revenue Management) to determine what the existing sales process, sales/success metrics, training programs, and KPIs are.

- Crowdsource a list of customer-facing conversations, talking points, pitches, marketing resources, case studies, call decks, objections to overcome, FAQs, etc. that are critical in the sales and service processes.
- Sketch out training plans and development paths by role.
- Document what you have heard and learned and present your findings with an initial recommendation to your leadership team.

The table below outlines a progression of goals and corresponding capabilities for your first 90 days. For a breakdown of the specific tasks that will help you achieve our recommended goals for your first 30, 60, and 90 days, please refer to the resources on our website: level213.com.

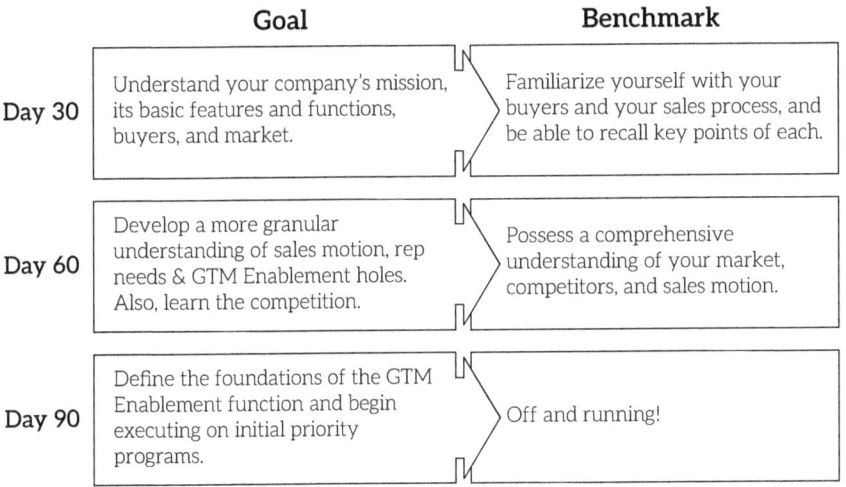

Figure 3.1: 30/60/90 Goals and benchmarks

Chapter 3 Debrief:
- Based on the current state of the GTM organization and the Enablement function at your company, which items in the 30/60/90 above are most relevant to you?
- Are there items you can think of that you would add to your own 30/60/90?

Applied Learning:
- Within each of your first three months, which five things will you start with to make the most headway?

Chapter 4:
Objectives and Metrics

For Enablement initiatives to have the most success, you must establish a clear purpose, defined outcomes, and ways to measure impact. Define and confirm with your stakeholders what the business needs to achieve and how you'll measure the results before the start of any enablement effort.

You need alignment on:
- **Terminal Objectives:** *What does the learner* **have to be able to do** *as a result of the enablement program?* This will dictate what they have to know and understand, and it will guide what you focus on in the programs.
- **Executable Objectives:** *What specific steps do they need to take to be able to accomplish the terminal objective?* This is the knowledge or skill set they can demonstrate and apply to achieve the terminal objectives.
- **Key Performance Indicators (KPIs):** *How will you measure the learning or impact of the enablement?* The KPIs and metrics should be determined up front with key stakeholders and should relate directly to the terminal and executable objectives. If you can, establish a pre-program baseline so you can track and compare the metrics and KPIs pre- and post-program and training rollout.

When all three aspects are present, each initiative can be tied to objectives and metrics that support agreed-upon goals that roll up into the broader GTM organization.

It is important to note that not all initiatives will have an entirely objective measure; some measures will be subjective. Things like time to ramp, time to first deal, days in stage, deal size, and sales cycle length are objective measures. Other items, like job satisfaction, engagement, etc., are more subjective. Both are important and deserve your consideration.

Related *Fueling the Revenue Engine* Podcast Episode:
- Episode 11: Metrics Driven Enablement

Chapter 4 Debrief:
- What examples have you seen of clearly defined objectives and metrics, and how do you think they contributed to the success of an enablement program or project?
- What do you see as the biggest challenges of adhering to clear objectives and metrics, and how can you take these into consideration in your planning and execution?

Applied Learning:
Pick one of your current programs or training opportunities and then apply the following inquiries:
- What would you define as the terminal objectives for this program?
- What would you define as the executable objectives for this program?
- Which KPIs do you think would be most meaningful and why?

Chapter 5:
Teaching Adults, Training Professionals

Why Adult Learning Is Different

Whether you are designing your own training or hiring an external professional for a specific topic, teaching/training is an essential part of enablement. One perhaps obvious fact to mention is that your "students" will be professional adults. This distinction is worth noting because when we think about teaching, we tend to rely on how we were taught as students in school, both in our younger years and perhaps even as adults. But learning in a work environment happens very differently than it does in a scholastic or academic one. There are specific traits of adult learners in a professional setting that you need to take into account as you design and deliver programs, since they affect engagement and knowledge retention. To this end, we want to familiarize you with Adult Learning Theory.

Adult Learning Theory

Professor of education Malcolm Shepherd Knowles pioneered the field of andragogy, or the art and science of how adults learn. His career spanned the mid-20th century, and his research forms the basis of today's Adult Learning Theory, which informs effective instructional design, a topic we'll explore in greater depth in the following chapters. He posited the following five assumptions about adult learners. The extent to which you design and deliver your programs in relation to these five assumptions will have a tremendous impact on how well your programs are received and implemented by the GTM team.

1. **Self-Concept**: As a person matures, their self-concept evolves from dependent personality toward self-directed human being. Knowing that your learners are driven by their own initiative helps you present information in ways that enroll and engage them as a group, while allowing for appropriate levels of individual autonomy.

2. **Adult Learner Experience**: As a person matures, they accumulate a growing reservoir of experience that becomes an increasing resource for learning. As trainers, we can capitalize on the knowledge our learners already have, but we also need to take into account the wide range of backgrounds that learners bring with them. The learning materials and activities we design must allow for a variety of different levels and types of previous experience.

3. **Readiness to Learn**: As a person matures, their readiness to learn becomes increasingly oriented to the developmental tasks of their social and professional roles. As you develop training programs, be mindful of how the training will benefit their role and be clear about what they will get out of the training. It is best practice to start a training session by stating: "**After this training, you will be able to...**" This ensures that the learner is intrinsically motivated to pay attention because they know how the knowledge will benefit them in their role.

4. **Orientation to Learning**: As a person matures, their time perspective changes from one of postponed application of knowledge to immediacy of application. As a result, all training sessions should include immediate application. The more closely related the application is to a real-life situation, the more intrinsically motivated the learner will be to participate, and the more likely they will be to retain the knowledge taught. This fact is particularly

important when designing programs for quota-driven professionals, who are taking time away from their revenue generating activities to complete the learning and have an understandably difficult time shifting into a learning rather than doing mode.

5. **Motivation to Learn**: As a person matures, their motivation to learn shifts from external to internal motivation. Similar to understanding your learners' self-concept, having an awareness of your learners' motivation to learn is critical for designing successful trainings. Enablement must think and design in nuanced ways that tap into more than just the external frameworks, guidelines, and rules; you need to harness your learners' own reasons for seeking out the knowledge you offer.

Key Principles for Applying Adult Learning Theory

As an adult yourself learning about learning, we can assume you'd like to apply this information as soon as possible. In the following chapters, we'll cover in depth a methodology for using Adult Learning Theory to design successful trainings. The foundation for doing so lies in the following three key principles:

- Experience (including mistakes) provides the basis for the learning opportunities. As adults, we learn more from our failures than from our successes. The opportunity to experiment with trial and error in a training exercise provides the time and experience needed to refine a new skill before applying it to a situation working with a real customer. In service of this goal, it's recommended to let your learner "fail forward" during a training experience, but this "failure" needs to be coupled with guidance, suggestions, and debrief from the facilitator in a safe space to ensure that the learning opportunity is captured.

Figure 5.1: Learning isn't linear

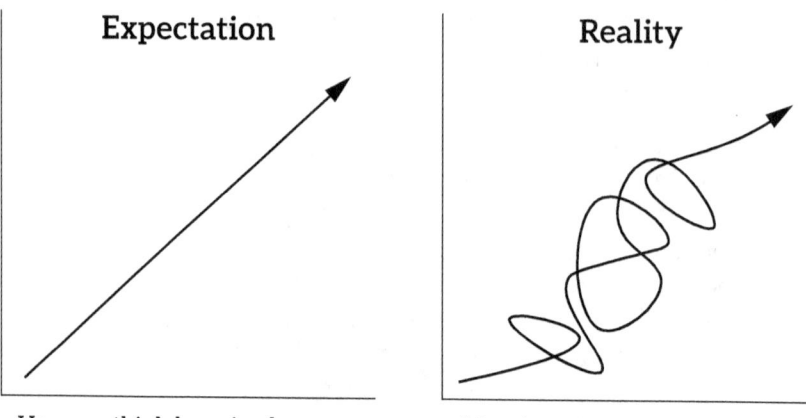

- Adults are most interested in learning subjects that have immediate relevance to and impact on their job or personal life.
- Adult learning is problem centered rather than content oriented. Knowledge dumps or "talk at you" slide-style presentations are not as effective as experiential training. This is not to say that you won't need to do a knowledge transfer section in a training, but that it should be primarily problem centered.

Traits of Adult Learners to Keep in Mind:
- **Preference for self-direction:** Adults feel the need to take responsibility for their lives and decisions; this is why it's important for them to have control over their learning. Therefore, self-assessment, multiple options, and initial yet subtle support are all imperative.
- **Less open minded:** Adults tend to be resistant to change. Maturity and profound life experiences can lead to rigidity, which is the enemy of learning. Thus, instructional designers need to provide a compelling "why" behind the change, present new concepts that can be linked to already established ones, and promote the need to explore.
- **Extensive personal experience:** Adults have lived longer, seen and done more, have a tendency to link their past

experiences to anything new, and validate new concepts based on prior learning. This is why it is extremely beneficial to form a class with adults who have similar levels of life experience, encourage discussion and sharing, and generally create a learning community with people who can interact in meaningful ways.

- **Multi-level responsibilities:** Your learners have a lot to juggle; they likely carry a quota and need to spend a majority of their time on revenue generating activities. This is why, even though training is absolutely crucial to prioritize, reps and revenue managers will find it difficult to make time for learning. Taking that into consideration, a GTM Enablement instructional designer needs to create programs that directly and positively impact the learners' productivity and development. The Enablement lead must be able to clearly articulate the purpose and importance of the program to management and reps alike, acknowledging their busy schedules and being mindful of when training is delivered or the time frame given for completion if the program is self-paced. A rule of thumb is to avoid rolling out a new training at the end of the quarter (or end of month if the business is sensitive to a monthly cadence) and try to avoid training during Q4 whenever possible. If you will be delivering instructor-led training, be mindful of prime sales and customer call times (time of day and/or day of week) when scheduling the live training sessions.
- **High expectations:** Customer-facing reps have high expectations. They want to be taught about things that will be useful to their work, expect to have immediate results, and will judge a course as "worth their while" or "a waste of time." As such, it's important to create a course that will highlight the advantages/benefits for them, meet their individual needs, and clearly address the learning challenges noted above.

Chapter 5 Debrief:
- What resonated with you the most about Adult Learning Theory?
- How does this awareness change your approach to training?
- Which elements of Adult Learning Theory do you find yourself challenged by in your own development?
- Do you think this is representative of the larger group you are working with? Why or why not?
- When have you seen training fall short (or even fail) because Adult Learning Theory concepts were not properly taken into consideration?
- Knowing what you do now, give an example of how the training could have been improved or adapted to be more effective.

Applied Learning:
Using one of your current programs, ask yourself:
- Where do you see the biggest challenges in incorporating Adult Learning Theory into this program?
- What will you specifically do to address each of the five assumptions?
- How will you apply the key principles as you build out the program?
- Given the groups you are working with, which of the adult learners' traits are most relevant and how will you address them?

Chapter 6:
Instructional Design Fundamentals

Designing Better Trainings

Now that we've established how adults learn, let's turn our attention to the art and science of skillfully designing training courses for Sales and Success teams. In other words, let's explore the field of instructional design.

Instructional design is the discipline of crafting optimal learning experiences. It spans the entire arc of effective teaching, from the initial planning of curricula, to the development of course structure and materials, through implementation of instructional activities. Simply put, instructional design is the rigorous thoughtfulness that makes learning as effective and enjoyable as possible.

Enablement professionals must approach instructional design through the lens of Adult Learning Theory in order to design training programs for sales reps that will maximize their engagement and knowledge retention. This chapter gives an overview of how to design a successful training program; we'll go into greater detail in Chapter 7 on each of the points noted.

When it comes to training courses, we've seen the good, the bad, and the ugly. The best ones follow a structure in which you clearly present objectives and then, for each objective:

1. Define the concepts
2. Teach the core knowledge to support each objective
3. Offer an example
4. Integrate knowledge using an application exercise
5. Assess retention of knowledge

Objectives

Objectives, or the desired competencies resulting from your training, come in two forms: terminal and executable. **Terminal objectives** are the actionable skill set the learner will acquire through your course; **executable objectives** are the discrete skills in that set. The best way to ensure that courses don't get too long or veer off topic is to build them around the objectives. If you find that some of your material doesn't support or align with your objectives, cut it from the course—or adjust the objectives if you believe this material is necessary vis-à-vis what the learner will need to be able to do as a result of the training. There can be several terminal objectives and likely several executable objectives, but keep in mind not to overwhelm your learner with too much at one time. Let **"what they need to be able to do as a result of the training"** be the guide to how many objectives there are. This metric will also dictate the length of the session.

Remember, begin every course in the following way: "After this session, you will be able to..."

- Terminal objectives
- Executables objectives

Useful objectives contain:
- Audience: whom the course is intended for
- Behavior: what the audience will be able to do as a result of the course
- Condition: when, where, or how the behavior is to be demonstrated

Clarify Your Objective

Your company is rolling out a new first call deck, and the Enablement team is designing training to teach the sales team how to use it. SMEs on the Product Marketing team tell you their objective is for the reps to "understand how to use the new call deck." While this is a common starting point (everyone wants the reps to understand how to use the deck), the work of defining and building a training requires objectives that are specific and actionable.

Think about what the learner has to actually do with the deck. How, when, and to whom will they present it? What will they have to say as they do so? How will their ability to perform their day-to-day job function vis-à-vis this deck be different/better as a result of your training? A successful training considers the *application of the understanding*. We'll explore in detail how to structure your training and optimize for application in the following chapters. For now, anchor your focus on what the learner has to be able to do as a result of the training.

An impactful objective would be: You (the learner) will be able to utilize the new first call deck as a tool to guide contextual discovery calls and uncover deeper levels of value with customers in the new vertical we are looking to gain market share in.

To give you a better sense for what you will likely encounter when building various training programs, let's look at a comparison of the common starting points for objectives vs. examples of curated learning objectives:

Figure 6.1: Common starting points vs. learning objectives

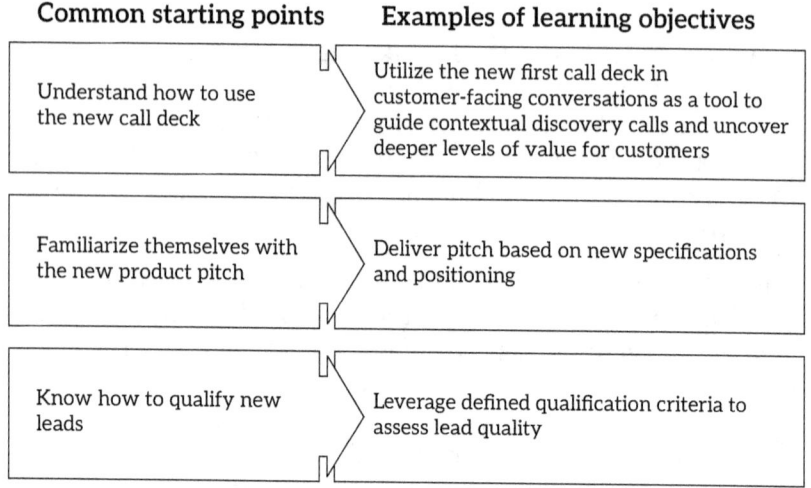

Once you establish your objectives, you need to design a program to support them. How you plan to deliver the training and the resources your organization has available will influence the tools and the format you use. An in-person course will very likely be based on a deck that holds the key points for your facilitation. If you are using asynchronous learning or a blended approach, you will most likely be designing within a learning management system (LMS).

Within the program, you'll need definitions, core concepts/skills, examples, and strategies for application—collectively, "the knowledge." To facilitate your course design process, we recommend you follow the remaining steps for each of your learning objectives, one by one:

- **Definition:** Define the concepts you are teaching in simple terms. This is important to establish a baseline for what is being taught, without the assumption that everyone understands the concept in the same way. For example, if you are teaching how to conduct sales prospecting, you must first define what prospecting is. Your definition would read something like "Sales prospecting is when sales development reps make outbound calls or send outbound emails to leads in hopes of cultivating opportunities for account executives. Prospecting can involve cold-calling as well as reaching out to nurture leads that have stopped responding to earlier communication." Note: In some cases it will make sense to include definitions at the beginning of a course to set the foundation of the meaning of terms or concepts. Other times, it makes more sense to include the definitions later in a course as a concept is introduced. Challenge yourself to leverage your knowledge of how adults learn to dictate where in your course the definition fits.

- **Prescription, Method, or Core Knowledge per Objective:** This section will be the core knowledge portion of the course, where you teach the skill or concepts needed to achieve the objectives. In the sales prospecting example above, this section would include things like whom to prospect to, how to conduct a cold call, how to write a prospecting email, etc. If the course is asynchronous, it is a good practice to either allow the learner to submit questions within the tool or hold office hours to field questions.
- **Example:** Providing an example of each method or skill taught is a critical component that allows the learner to connect the dots of how the content of the course applies to the day-to-day motion of their job. Examples are key to knowledge retention. Place the example in the context of how the learner will actually use the content they are learning. This could look like providing talking points for a phone call (or email) when teaching how to do sales prospecting. Sometimes using an additional counterexample, something not to do or that doesn't work, can be a powerful reinforcement of your primary example. Consider this method if you want to impart a skill that you often see executed incorrectly.
- **Exercise/Application:** Now have the learner apply what they learned. Provide exercises that allow the learner to practice and reinforce the skills/concepts.
    - Remember, adults learn by doing and have a desire to apply information immediately.
    - This section should be as experiential as possible and take up the majority of your allotted time for the training session.

- You may wish to include multiple examples and exercises as knowledge checks throughout the course, building on concepts and assessing multiple skills as needed to achieve the learning objectives. These exercises are intended to prompt the learner to combine what they've learned and demonstrate their ability to execute on the course objectives.
- Don't make the application too easy. Letting a learner "fail forward" in a safe training environment will solidify the learning and support recall of the knowledge when they go to apply it to a real scenario in their role.
- Continuing our sales prospecting example above, in the application section, have the participants do prospecting research, draft and send real prospecting emails, role-play customer conversation scenarios, and/or even conduct live cold calls utilizing the methods you taught.
- Tip: Always schedule more time than you think you need for activities. Giving learners time and space to work within the learning curve and to hone their skills is vital to their development. This time also allows them to digest the material and start to think through and road test the practical application. To anchor the experience, always debrief after they have completed the activity. This ensures understanding and provides an opportunity to discuss questions or struggles that may have come up during the activity portion.

- **Assessment:** Finally, assess their knowledge of what they were taught. Make sure to create assessment questions that allow the learners to demonstrate their ability and proficiency in fulfilling the learning objectives. Your assessments will often be a mix of a quiz and role-plays or live demos, depending on the defined objectives and outcomes of the course. Continuing our example of a sales prospecting course, you would assess that they can complete proper customer research, write a prospecting email, and conduct a prospecting call. If the course includes a certification, the learner would receive their certification after successfully completing the assessment(s).

- **Note:** In some cases, organizations will allow learners to "test out" of taking the course. If the learner has previous training on the topic, it may make sense to have them take the assessment prior to the course. If they achieve a 100% score, they have demonstrated that they have the knowledge they need to execute on this topic and have met the terminal and executable objectives. Under these circumstances, there is no need for them to take the course. If you are teaching something new that you know they could not have learned previously (for example, if you have a specific way you want them to conduct prospecting and it is being designed and rolled out for the first time), then it is best not to offer a "test out" option.

Related *Fueling the Revenue Engine* Podcast Episode:
- Episode 6: Designing Training for Salespeople

Chapter 6 Debrief:
- What resonated with you the most about defining objectives?
- How do you think clearly defined objectives support learners in their ability to engage in a training program?
- When you look at the elements that follow the objectives (Definition, Prescription, Example, Exercise, Assessment), where do you typically see training programs fall short?
- What impact do the missing or incomplete elements have on learning and engagement?

Applied Learning:
Using one of your current programs in the early stages of planning:
- Follow the steps outlined above and sketch out an outline for the program that includes Objectives, Definition, Prescription, Example, Exercise, and Assessment. Using the outline as your guide:
    - Draft terminal and executable objectives in the "After this session, you will be able to..." format.
    - Identify concepts that need to have definitions created for them.
    - Determine what you will include in the prescription section.
    - Define what types of examples you would like to use.
    - List several types of appropriate exercises you could incorporate into the program.
    - Create a first draft of an assessment.
- Look back over your outline and the information you have included, and as yourself:
    - Which parts are you confident you can continue to develop effectively?
    - For which parts do you need additional clarification and/or support to develop the program?

Chapter 7:
Designing Learning Objectives

Now that we've established the importance of clearly defined objectives and presented an overview of how to build a training around your objectives, let's dig into the specifics of objectives—how they can differ from each other—and why that matters. Understanding how adult learners process different types of new information will help you optimize the design of your trainings. The first step is classifying your objectives by what level of competency they require to be achieved.

Tools for Classifying Learning Objectives

The most helpful rubric we've found for designing GTM enablement trainings comes from the field of education. Twentieth-century educational psychologist Benjamin Bloom designed a hierarchical framework, known as Bloom's Taxonomy, to classify learning objectives into progressive levels of complexity and specificity (Bloom, 1956). For the past 75 years, scholars have attempted to improve upon or modernize Bloom's schema, but no such revisions have been as impactful as the original taxonomy. Bloom's explanation of how we acquire knowledge remains the gold standard for

Figure 7.1: Bloom's Taxonomy

```
                    /\
                   /  \
                  /CREATE\       Produce new or original work
                 /--------\      Design, assemble, construct, conjecture, develop,
                /          \     formulate, author, investigate
               /  EVALUATE  \    Justify a stand or decision
              /--------------\   Appraise, argue, defend, judge, select, support,
             /                \  value, critique, weigh
            /     ANALYZE      \ Draw connections among ideas
           /--------------------\Differentiate, organize, relate, compare, contrast,
          /                      \distinguish, examine, experiment, question, test
         /         APPLY          \Use information in new situations
        /--------------------------\Execute, implement, solve, use, demonstrate,
       /                            \interpret, operate, schedule, sketch
      /         UNDERSTAND           \Explain ideas or concepts
     /--------------------------------\Classify, describe, discuss, explain, identify,
    /                                  \locate, recognize, report, select, translate
   /            REMEMBER                \Recall facts and basic concepts
  /--------------------------------------\Define, duplicate, list, memorize,
                                           repeat, state
```

instructional design and is thus the basis of our training design framework.

Bloom's Taxonomy outlines seven levels of competency, which are named for what the learner is able to do within each. The levels climb like a ladder, from most accessible to most challenging; to advance to a higher level, you must be competent in the skills that define the preceding level. Bloom's Taxonomy also provides guidelines for how to assess whether or not the learner possesses a given level's requisite knowledge, and we'll explore assessments in the next chapter. In this chapter, we're examining how to ensure that your courses and programs follow the instructional design framework we have already outlined.

To start creating your objectives, you must determine which level (or levels) of competency the training fits. Look at your goals and consider what the learner should be able to do upon completion of the training. The majority of the courses you create will fit into the first three levels: Remember,

Understand or Apply. These three stages are the fundamentals of training anyone on a new concept or skill. If you are working with a very mature workforce, you may also end up designing material at the Analyze, Evaluate, and/or Create levels, but we find that the vast majority of the programs we create fit into the first three.

How you present the information you need to convey and the specific language you employ, especially the verbs you use in reference to your objectives, are critically important. So too are the types of assessments you create. Working with Bloom's Taxonomy allows you to be highly intentional in your instructional design. And intentionality correlates strongly with success. Let's take a closer look at the three levels you will work with the most:

- **Remember level** is used when the learner has to recall basic concepts but does not yet have to explain or apply the knowledge.
    - For example, if you are introducing new rules of engagement (ROE), reps will need to *remember* them but will not likely have to explain them to anyone.
    - An example of an appropriate verb to use in defining the executable objective is "After this training, you will be able to recall the rules of engagement for reaching out to prospects." Note, a follow-up objective could include application, but for the purposes of this example, we are laying the foundation of recalling what the rules are, not how to apply them yet.
    - To assess that a learner remembers the ROE, you could test them via multiple choice or matching, because it is okay for them to see a list to remind them of the correct answer.
- **Understand level** is used when the learner needs to explain the concept(s) to others.
    - A rep who has to *explain* (appropriate verb in this case) the pain points addressed by your product to a customer will need to be trained how to do this in the Understand level.
    - Your objective should read "After this training, you will be able to explain the pain points addressed by our product to a customer."

- You can assess their ability to do this by having them write out the pain points addressed by each product set and describe (another Understand level verb) the value of the product.
- **Apply level** is used when the learner has to use the information in new situations.
  - For example, a rep needs to demo the product. To do so, they will need to *demonstrate* the features and execute the functions of the product.
  - Your objective could state, "After this training, you will be able to demo the product."
  - An appropriate assessment would be requiring the rep to record themselves conducting a demo.

Training Design Guidelines for Differing Levels and Objectives

When designing training and using the "what does the learner need to be able to do?" guideline, you'll see that each level has a very different expectation in terms of ability to execute. The table below lays out some specific verbs to use when asking your learners to engage with your subject matter, depending on the Bloom's level. It also includes our recommendations for how to present the training content needed to achieve your objectives.

For example, if you are designing a training for Understand level objectives, you might instruct your learners by comparing two pieces of information. And you might illustrate that comparison with a diagram. Refer to the table to see all our recommendations for verbs and instructional aids that correspond appropriately to the Bloom's levels. Deliberate word choice and thoughtfully designed content will significantly enrich the knowledge training portion of your course and facilitate greater knowledge retention.

Although most of the courses you will create belong in the Remember, Understand, and/or Apply levels, at some point your training objectives may lie within the Analyze, Evaluate, and Create levels, so we include support for designing trainings in those groups as well. Be careful to avoid using higher-level

Figure 7.2: Suggested Verbs and Media by Level

Level	Verbs	Ways to Convey Content
Remember	list, name, recall, record, relate, repeat, state, tell, underline	definitions, dictionaries, events, articles, recordings, supplemental resources
Understand	compare, describe, discuss, explain, express, identify, recognize, restate, tell, translate	comparisons, diagrams, graphs, outlines, photographs, posters, stories, summaries, recordings
Apply	apply, complete, construct, demonstrate, dramatize, employ, illustrate, interpret, operate, practice, schedule, sketch, use	diagrams, videos, graphics, lists, photographs, case studies
Analyze	analyze, appraise, categorize, compare, contrast, debate, differentiate, distinguish, examine, experiment, inspect, inventory, measure, test	models, graphs, reports, questionnaires, surveys, analyses of perspectives, conclusions
Evaluate	appraise, argue, arrange, assemble, assess, collect, combine, compare, conclude, estimate, evaluate, interpret, judge, justify, manage, measure, organize, plan, prepare, propose, rate, select, score	articles, books, conclusions, experiments, games, reports, stories
Create	choose, complete, compose, construct, create, design, devise, formulate, revise	conclusions, editorials, group discussions, evaluations, surveys

verbs and content formats if they aren't appropriate for your objectives.

Note: Although we have followed the "Remember" and "Understand" naming conventions for the first two levels of Bloom's Taxonomy, these levels are also commonly referred to as "Knowledge" and "Comprehend." If other sources citing Bloom refer to "Knowledge," it can be used interchangeably with "Remember." Similarly, "Comprehend" is equivalent to "Understand."

Chapter 7 Debrief:
- What was most impactful about Bloom's Taxonomy, and how will it inform the way you build programs?
- Which verbs resonate with you as especially useful for the training programs coming up next on your priority list?

Applied Learning:
Using one of your current programs:
- Ask yourself: What levels of Bloom's Taxonomy does this program belong to?
- Edit/refine your original objectives utilizing verbs and supportive ways to convey content that correspond with the appropriate level(s).

Chapter 8:
Assessing Outcomes

Bloom's Taxonomy provides an integral structure for designing trainings and also serves as a powerful tool to assess how well your learners have absorbed the subject matter. Assessing your learners also helps you determine which ones are ready to move on and which are in need of further instruction. As we mentioned in the previous chapter, most of the trainings you will create will fall into Bloom's Remember, Understand, and/or Apply levels. Let's look at how to assess knowledge at these levels.

All About Assessments

The form an assessment takes and the items it covers should reflect the purpose of the training and its desired outcomes (behaviors based on newfound competencies). It's best practice to create the assessment plan or criteria immediately following the creation of objectives, before building out the rest of the training. Creating the assessment concurrently with the objectives helps sharpen your focus on the objectives, providing a clear end point as you develop the ensuing course content.

Assessments come in many forms, but *assessment items must be congruent with the objectives being assessed*. And the number of objectives assessed should take into consideration the acceptable adequate performance of the learner. In other words, what do you need to know about a learner's competence to be confident they can execute on the training's objective(s)?

Most learning management systems have the ability to issue assessments (of all degrees of complexity) following a course, so learners can complete them asynchronously. If you're delivering a live training, your assessment could occur as part of the training, e.g., a live pitch certification with someone scoring delivery against a rubric. You might also choose to utilize a hybrid approach, assigning an online assessment after a live session. In other cases, you could have a live assessment after an asynchronous training. When determining the assessment format, keep in mind that you will need to reference and score the assessment. Depending on the volume of responses, sometimes old-fashioned pen and paper is appropriate, and other times a digital record of each participant's submission is helpful. Regardless of the format, always make sure your assessment is measuring the learners' grasp of the objectives and the content. How you choose to assess is a function of the objectives you're assessing, how you prefer to evaluate responses, how scalable you need the assessment to be, and how you want to engage with your learners.

Assessing by Level

The complexity of the assessments you need to design will vary based on the Bloom's level of the learning objectives in your trainings. No matter the level, assessment questions must be ordered and worded as the content was taught. Your goal is to ascertain your learners' competence, not to confuse them. Avoid "trick questions."

To design skillful assessments, use verbs that correspond to the Bloom's level you're assessing. Refer to Figure 7.2 in the previous chapter for a list of verbs by level. Verbs are action words, so to assess your learners' mastery of the objective, they should be able to act as the verbs suggest. If, for example, a Remember-level objective of your training was for a rep to "name the seven elements of a request for information," the assessment should use a Remember-level verb and ask the learner to *select the seven elements from a list*. At every level, order and word your assessments as the content was taught.

When assessing Remember-level material, you'll want to rely primarily on **selected response** format questions, which allow the learner to select a single best choice from a list of possibilities, known as a "convergent answer." Because you're delivering content that simply needs to be recalled, not interpreted, Remember-level assessment questions don't need to demand arduous thinking. Selected response questions such as true/false, matching, or multiple choice allow you to verify efficiently whether or not your learners have grasped the objective(s). One note of caution, however: true/false answers should be used sparingly, since they are subject to a 50% correct guess rate. Use a variety of selected response options to assess Remember-level objectives.

To assess understanding of the more sophisticated or nuanced aspects of your training's objective(s), information belonging to the Understand level of Bloom's taxonomy, you need to know that your learner can do more than select a convergent answer. You need them to be able to interpret and synthesize the knowledge. Because the stakes are generally higher, assessments for Understand-level objectives demand especially thoughtful design. Use **constructed response** format assessments such as short answer questions that ask the learner to compare, describe, or discuss the training material in their own words, a task that places a higher demand on memory and reasoning. You'll likely choose to have them articulate their thoughts in writing or record a video submission.

Assessments of Apply-level material need to do just that: ask the learner to apply what they've learned. A demonstration of knowledge in practice is termed **performed response**. You may ask the learner to give a presentation or to participate in a role-play interaction—either live, simulated, or with an actual customer. And you may ask them to complete some more challenging constructed response questions. These Apply-level assessments help you determine which learners are ready for

Figure 8.1: General outline of assessment types by Bloom's level

---

Remember
- Purpose: Assess for recall of factual information, concepts, and discrete skills
- Approach: Selected and/or constructed response
- Example: True/false

Understand
- Purpose: Assess for ability to restate material in their own words and recognize new examples of training concepts
- Approach: Constructed response
- Example: Written response

Apply
- Purpose: Assess for ability to apply knowledge and demonstrate learned skills in context
- Approach: Performed response
- Example: Role play

---

new material and which ones may need more support and/or should review the information previously presented. They also allow you to compare the learners' abilities against established field standards, as well as same-level peers.

The correlation between a given Bloom's level and an assessment approach is not a concrete rule but rather a general guideline. There will be times that a Remember-level objective may need a constructed response assessment. Similarly, an Apply-level objective may occasionally warrant a constructed response assessment as well. We encourage you to design assessments with flexibility, staying mindful of your ultimate objective: to gather actionable data about how well your learners have grasped the training objective(s).

Post Training Surveys

Once the training is delivered, you'll want to gather objective feedback on the content and its delivery. Post-training surveys are often referred to, somewhat cynically, as "happy sheet feedback forms" and ask things like "How would you rate the instructor, the content delivered, etc.?" In other words, were you happy with the training? While that feedback might be of interest to the facilitator, it doesn't provide any insight into how effective the training was or whether or not the objectives were met. Happy sheets tend to get scored by participants based on how much they like the facilitator personally or enjoyed the training, which are subjective measures and rarely reflect the outcome, i.e., the skills imparted or value received from completing the course.

We need objective measurements to know whether or not we've made an impact. An assessment needs to avoid subjectivity to accurately determine the learner's feelings about what they've learned and whether they'll be able to utilize the knowledge you set out to teach them. To assess your learners' grasp of the objectives you presented, use a five-point scale to collect feedback.

The five most useful categories to assess are:
- **Agreement** with a description of post-training ability. The learner is ranking the degree to which they agree that they have learned something useful and applicable.
- **Frequency** of use for a given skill post-training. The learner is ranking the degree of frequency with which they predict they will use the new skill they have learned.
- **Importance** of a given aspect of the training. The learner is ranking the degree of importance that they feel the new skill has for them/their work.
- **Quality** of a given aspect of the facilitator. The learner is ranking the degree of excellence of the facilitator's instruction.
- **Likelihood** of using an aspect of the training. The learner is ranking the degree of probability that they will use the new skill they have learned.

For each of these categories, the scale of response that you want to measure ranges within these five options:
1. Extremely positive
2. Somewhat positive
3. Neutral
4. Somewhat negative
5. Extremely negative

Figure 8.2: Categories of assessment questions with five-point feedback scale responses

Category	Example Question	Five-Point Responses
Agreement	I am confident in my ability to demo the product to a customer.	1. Strongly agree 2. Agree 3. Undecided 4. Disagree 5. Strongly disagree
Frequency	I will use the product demo training I received. (post-training 6-weeks)	1. Always 2. Usually 3. About half the time 4. Seldom 5. Never
Importance	The level of importance of the product demo training is:	1. Very important 2. Important 3. Moderately important 4. Of little importance 5. Unimportant
Quality	The quality of the facilitator's knowledge was:	1. Excellent 2. Above average 3. Average 4. Below average 5. Extremely poor
Likelihood	The likelihood that I will use the demo product training I received is:	1. To a great extent 2. Somewhat 3. Undecided 4. Very little 5. Not at all

You will need to adapt these variations to suit the categories you are assessing. We include examples of assessment questions and responses below.

Responding to Feedback

In addition to the assessment results themselves, the feedback you've solicited/acquired from your learners is a valuable data set supplying answers to the question: How well did this training go? Positive feedback indicates the aspects of your course that were well received by the learners, suggesting that you continue to offer similar topics or tactics in the future. Less positive feedback helps you identify where you may need to provide additional reinforcement or supplemental training on certain topics. In some cases, it may suffice to adjust the existing content slightly; in others, you may need to redesign the training with additional resources and/or consider offering follow-up trainings.

Chapter 8 Debrief:
- What criteria will you use to plan your assessment approach?
- What do you think the most difficult part of creating meaningful post-training surveys will be?

Applied Learning:
Using one of your current programs in early stages of planning:
- Create an initial draft of an assessment based on the guidelines above.
- Draft a post-training survey based on the guidelines above.

Chapter 9:
Subject Matter Experts, Knowledge Engineering, and Course Facilitation

We're ready now to address the actual building of training content. As we mentioned in the introduction of this book, GTM enablement professionals are the curators who gather all the information the GTM teams need to do their job. Much of the curation process involves knowledge engineering, the process of distilling the information and expertise held by subject matter experts (SMEs) and then re-packaging it into tools and resources that the revenue generating teams can leverage in their efforts to win, retain, and/or expand business for the company.

Typical SMEs you work with are:
- Product managers
- Product Marketing
- Sales/Success managers
- Sales/Success reps
- Legal
- Finance
- Industry experts

In most cases, the SMEs hold a tremendous amount of knowledge about the product or service being sold, the market landscape, competitive intel, internal processes, etc. Even with the expertise they hold, they typically don't have the time or the level of instructional design background needed to curate and deliver this information in a way that's useful to the customer-facing teams. This gap is the space you and your instructional design skills need to bridge.

Knowledge Engineering

In many cases the SME will deliver the knowledge training portion of the course, but Enablement remains responsible for orchestrating the presentation in accordance with instructional design best practices. SMEs are so deeply steeped in all they know about a topic that they need your instructional design expertise to organize the content in such a way that learners can effectively engage with it and be able to leverage it after the training is complete. Put simply, the SME holds the knowledge but likely needs your guidance to re-package it. The first step in this process is to complete knowledge engineering as the basis for the course design.

Start by setting up time to conduct knowledge engineering sessions with the appropriate SME. These sessions are critical to ensure that the relevant content is accurately sourced. Don't skimp on this step for fear of "taking up the SME's time." It's often more time consuming for you and the SME to have to go back and fix something that was misrepresented to begin with.

Notice your own orientation to the topic you'll be researching and teaching. You'll often find that you are responsible for distilling content on a topic you know very little about. While this disconnect can feel intimidating or overwhelming, it's actually a big advantage in the curation process. Because you are not holding any preconceived ideas about a given topic, you're able to leverage a state of unbiased curiosity, sometimes called "beginner's mind." Being unfamiliar with the topic also puts you in a position similar to that of the learners you will be training. *Being positioned on the outside of understanding affords you better insight into the questions learners might have, as well as the explanations and examples they will benefit from.* Conversely, even if you think you know a lot about the topic, approach your meeting with the SME with sincere curiosity. Make sure to get all the topic-specific details directly from them so you don't miss important nuances that the learners will need.

Ask questions of the SMEs and document all the knowledge they have to share. Start with the most important question: **"What do the reps have to be able to do with the knowledge to be more proficient within their roles?"** This question will help you parse out the learning objectives and ensure that you extract all the knowledge needed to hit those objectives. Next, ask the SME to define the components of the topic you are discussing. You may think this step is obvious or redundant, but clear and consistent definitions will help ensure that you and the SME are communicating accurately, and that the learners ultimately acquire the understanding of the topic as intended. You'll use the SME's definitions in your course, as discussed in the instructional design framework (Chapter 6).

- Think of yourself as a detective when asking questions of the SME, and put yourself in the place of the learner audience. What questions would the learner have? What objections would they have? Where will they need very prescriptive direction? What examples would connect the dots for them in terms of learning content and then using the knowledge to do their jobs? Be very thorough as you compile the data needed to design the course.

Although you are taking the lead to design the course, whenever possible the SME should be a partner with you, especially if they will be part of the facilitation team. Once you have completed the initial knowledge engineering and have the raw materials you need, you'll start constructing the course. As you build, be sure to get input and feedback from the SME to confirm that your representation of the information is accurate. When you've completed the design, be sure the SME reviews the content for accuracy and have them assist in creating the exercise/application portions, as well as some of the assessment questions.

Content Facilitation

GTM enablement professionals spend a lot of time delivering training in several different modes that include in person, live virtual, and asynchronous training. While facilitation differs slightly based on the delivery mode, there are some basic guidelines to keep in mind for all training.

What you need to do:
- Structure your training using the instructional design principles detailed earlier in this book.
- Pre-training prep and rehearsals: Always rehearse content delivery for live or live virtual sessions. Anyone who is going to be "in front of the room" must rehearse. That includes you and your co-presenters. The purpose of the rehearsal is to practice saying the content out loud to make sure it rolls off the tongue correctly, time the sessions to give you an idea of how long content will take to go over, and ensure that everyone is 100% ready for a live delivery.
- Time management is important no matter the training delivery mode. *Training always takes longer than you anticipate.* Always book more time than you think you need for the training, especially the exercise portions. For self-paced training modules, give your learners realistic (liberally padded) expectations of how long each module will take to complete.
- Manage the classroom (in person or virtual) for live training. At times you will be the sole presenter, but very often you will co-present with SMEs. If you are co-facilitating, it's best practice for you to kick off the training and go over the learning objectives before turning it over to the SME to deliver the content. You should also facilitate the exercises, debriefs, reflections, and wrap up the session, all while keeping time and ensuring that the participants are engaged.
- For longer training sessions, keep in mind that you will need to structure breaks so learners can get up and move, use the restroom, refill beverages, or eat snacks. In general, two hours is the maximum amount of training time we recommend before offering a break. If your

training is scheduled to run all day long, you will need to account for lunch, as well as morning and afternoon breaks. All food for in person training should be provided on site so learners aren't leaving the primary training area and aren't beholden to crowded restaurants or long service wait times.

Considerations for live virtual training:

Live virtual training provides a scalable, affordable, and convenient option to provide live training without everyone having to be in the same physical space. While this delivery method provides some added benefits, it also introduces some challenges that will need to be navigated.

- Since you are not in control or fully aware of the environment the learner is in, you do not have insight into what else is competing for their attention. People are very conditioned to "multitask" while in virtual meetings. To combat this tendency, structure the session to leverage engagement tools such as chat discussions, polls, breakout groups, and collaborative whiteboards that keep participants engaged and focused on the learning.
- It's harder to stay focused on a virtual session. For longer sessions, you may want to include more breaks than you would for in-person sessions. We have found a crisp five-minute break at the top of every hour works well, but stick to a prompt break start and end time, or you'll lose out on valuable session time.
- If you are adapting something that would have been a full day or a multi-day in person session, you will need to break it up into shorter sessions over multiple days. Expecting someone to be engaged and effective on a virtual session for an entire day is unrealistic.
  - We have found a maximum of four hours on a virtual session (with short breaks every hour) works best for longer sessions. For example, what used to be a single day-long training or working session turns into two half-day sessions. This also means you will need to do a brief recap of the first session as your introduction to the second session to ensure everyone is up to speed.

- Having a co-host to handle engagement and logistics is very helpful. This allows the main presenter (you, the SME, or perhaps a third party) to focus on delivering the content while the co-host manages any technical challenges a learner might face, keeps track of chat discussions, manages breakout rooms, tracks time, etc. No matter your role during the live training, having a division of labor affords you better command of the virtual room than you would have if you were the only host/facilitator.
- Take time zones of all participants into account. While virtual sessions mean we can have people from different geographic locations on one call, we also need to be mindful of planning around mealtimes, early mornings, late evenings, etc. for each time zone. This is critical to ensure that all learners can stay engaged for the entire session.
- Whenever possible, record the sessions so you can get more scalability out of the live event. You can use the recording (or portions of it) for follow-up reinforcement and just-in-time access by the learners. Recordings are also very helpful for the Enablement team to review what worked well and what needs to be improved for future sessions.

Live training materials that you will need to create for each training:

- **Training Deck:** This is the actual course content that gets delivered, often in Google Slides or Microsoft PowerPoint format.
- **Participant Guides:** These guides include notes, general timing of sections, prompts to complete exercises, and any relevant graphics, resources, or context needed for the learner. They can be printed for in-person events or shared in virtual document format for learners to access on their laptops.
- **Facilitator Guides:** Include everything the participant gets in the Participant Guide, with additional notes, contextual information, and timing prompts for the facilitators and co-presenters.

Asynchronous training materials that you will need to create for each training:
- **Training Course:** This is the actual course content that gets delivered, usually in a learning management system.
- **Knowledge Checks:** These are the practice activity/application exercises.

Training delivery guidelines applicable to both live sessions and asynchronous training videos:
- Keep it engaging.
- Use different learning styles.
- Don't read the slides—teach the slides.
- Vary the way content is presented, e.g., highlighted call-outs, slide transitions, animations, flip cards, etc.
- Signpost often by letting people know where they are in the course and where the lessons are going.
- Use stories and analogies.
- Reinforce the "why" through contextual examples of how something applies to the learner's role or the outcome they can achieve.
- For breakout activities, clearly explain what you want participants to do, why, and how much time you're allotting them.

Time management guidelines for live sessions (in person or virtual):
- This is your participant's time; you are just the timekeeper.
- Start on time and end on time.
- Explore and encourage discovery, but don't let distractions and tangents take over.
- Create a "parking lot" for questions.
  - You may be tempted to take questions as they come up, but taking questions can derail your flow and time management. If the course was designed correctly, all the questions should be answered as you unfold the content.
  - Let the learners know up front that you will not be taking questions during the knowledge delivery but that you have set Q&A prompts throughout the session.

- For live virtual sessions, encourage questions in the chat. This allows you and the co-host to get a sense of the questions without having to derail the session delivery to respond to each question asked. As you monitor the chat, you can decide when the best time will be to address the questions. It is also a good practice to have the SME for the topic monitor the chat. This allows them to respond to quick questions as they come in. Questions that are relevant to the entire group or that need more explanation can be addressed during designated Q&A prompts in the session.
  - Make sure to include ample time for Q&A breaks at the appropriate times during the session.
  - Agree on break times and stick to them.

These are long lists, but don't worry, we'll be going into more detail on how to design and deliver quality trainings in the next chapter.

Chapter 9 Debrief:

The following questions are designed as inquiries to inform how you plan for and conduct your knowledge engineering.

- In what ways can you incorporate instructional design best practices when working with SMEs to create training content?
- How can adopting a "beginner's mindset" help you to anticipate learner questions and needs more effectively?
- What strategies will you use with SMEs to facilitate effective knowledge engineering?

Applied Learning:

Using one of your current programs in early stage development:

- Ask yourself: Which SMEs do you need to set up knowledge engineering sessions with?
- Create an initial draft of the training deck.
- Based on the content, sketch out an initial training timeline (remember the guidelines above for time management).

Chapter 10:
Designing and Delivering a Complete Program

Well-designed training programs do much more than effectively deliver content. The best trainings follow a three-phase planning model, and only one phase is dedicated to introducing the training's content to learners.

Phase 1: Pre-session Work

Training often begins before the training event. In order for your learners to maximize their experience in a given session, you often need to engage with them before the actual event to be sure they have the appropriate foundational understanding. If your learners don't have a strong background in topics relevant to the upcoming training, you can assign them what's commonly referred to as "pre-work." Typically brief and not overly complicated, the purpose is to ensure all participants are starting with a shared context and similar levels of preparation coming into the training event. You may be introducing a topic for the first time, or perhaps offering a short refresher on previously trained relevant content. In either case, common examples of pre-work include reading an article, reviewing a case study, and/or studying a deal that will be referenced in the training. The more you can prime your learners for what's to come, the more they will take away from the training event itself.

Phase 2: Learning Event

This phase is where the actual training takes place, whether live or asynchronous. The training in this phase builds on the pre-work, introduces new concepts as part of the core knowledge transfer, and provides the structure for initial practice.

Phase 3: Follow-up and Coaching

Training doesn't end at the end of your learning event. Successful training includes follow-up, coaching, training reinforcement, practice, and/or learning integration that follow the learning event.

While it's tempting to focus entirely on Phase 2 and shortchange the planning and follow-up phases, you do so to your detriment. For participants to realize the full potential of a learning event, they must come in prepared (Phase 1) and remain engaged afterward (Phase 3). A critical responsibility of Enablement (in partnership with the rep's FLM) is to maintain the momentum of Phase 2 by building a robust Phase 3 that lets participants practice and apply what they've learned. They also need opportunities to engage in follow-up activities and receive coaching on the learning objectives.

Leadership experts Jack Zenger, Joe Folkman, and Robert Sherwin first identified stunning results in 2005 regarding the three phases of learning, particularly the impact of Phase 3: Follow-up and Coaching (Zenger et al. 2005). Through their research over the last two decades, Zenger, Folkman and Sherwin make an impressive case for practice and learning integration, or what they call "The Promise of Phase Three."

Their research shows, and our experience supports, that 50% of the value of any learning event or training program is realized in the post-training follow-up work. Despite these compelling findings, organizations typically invest 10% of their resources in Phase 1, 85% in Phase 2, and only 5% in Phase 3.

Resource allocation is beginning to shift across the technology sector, with many organizations now noticing the impact of follow-up and changing their prioritization accordingly.

Beyond Coaching: Micro Learning Objects

Coaching is critical (and we'll explore it in Part Two of this book), but it's often insufficient as the sole mechanism of training-specific follow-up. To effectively reinforce the key learnings of training content, we recommend that you include micro learning objects (MLOs) paired with coaching as part of your Phase 3 design. MLOs can also be leveraged as Phase 1 pre-work when a previous training is relevant to an upcoming session. When determining which skills and content need to be reinforced, return to your key learning objectives and then set a schedule for delivering MLOs.

Depending on the needs and availability of your reps, you might opt to share MLOs in brief biweekly or monthly deep dive training sessions, either live or asynchronous. For the greatest impact, we recommend that you cover only one skill or topic per session and that each session include application practice. To be most effective, these sessions should be short and focused, providing an opportunity to discuss real-life application of the knowledge that your learners acquired during the learning event and have actually used since. Be sure to leave time for questions and reflections.

If offering a session isn't possible, you can also deliver MLOs by email, Slack, or other internal messaging platform. Schedule a series of short reminders/refreshers of key concepts to go out on a regular basis. As with MLO sessions, limit each message to one skill or topic from the original training. You will help your learners recall the training more effectively if you add context and framing language to the concept you are seeking to reinforce. Include assessment quizzes with each part of the MLO release to measure retention of the content where applicable.

LEVEL+ Framework

We believe so strongly in the efficacy of sound instructional design and the three phases of learning to drive revenue that

Figure 10.1: Level+ framework

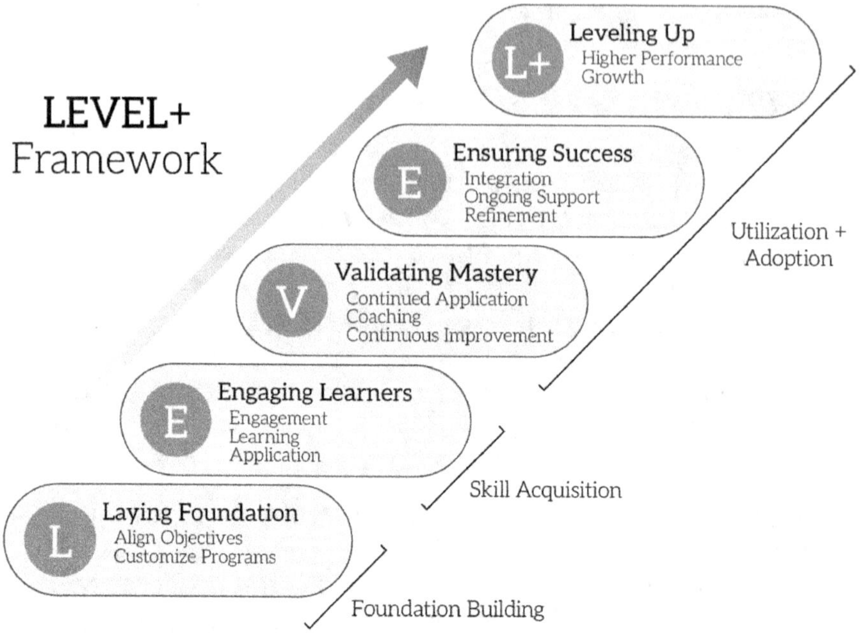

LEVEL+ Framework

- **L+ Leveling Up** — Higher Performance, Growth
- **E Ensuring Success** — Integration, Ongoing Support, Refinement
- **V Validating Mastery** — Continued Application, Coaching, Continuous Improvement
- **E Engaging Learners** — Engagement, Learning, Application
- **L Laying Foundation** — Align Objectives, Customize Programs

Utilization + Adoption
Skill Acquisition
Foundation Building

we developed our own framework to help our clients create best in class enablement programs. We call this framework LEVEL+.

LEVEL+ ensures that Enablement-designed programs will progress sequentially through the three learning phases: establishing foundational understanding, imparting new skills, and applying/integrating these new skills into routine practice. Our Foundation Building phase is the first area of focus; it correlates to Zenger, Folkman, and Sherwin's "pre-work" phase. Here we help clients clearly define their objectives and establish the necessary shared understanding of the initiative among all relevant parties. With that common ground established, we move into Skill Acquisition (correlating to the main learning event), where we make use of highly engaging content, informed by our extensive instructional design experience, to train our clients' teams on necessary skills. In our final phase, Utilization + Adoption (correlating to follow-up), client teams practice their new learning, hone their understanding, and incorporate the new skills into their job function. With this approach, trained skills become mastered knowledge. The LEVEL+ framework consistently delivers tangible business results (increased retention, revenue growth, optimized customer engagement, and better customer experiences, among other KPIs), as well as increased confidence across the team. We take pride in seeing teams take themselves to the next level of revenue generation effectiveness, and with LEVEL+ we see this motion solidified and accelerated.

For support with building enablement programs following the LEVEL+ protocol, you can reach us at level213.com/contact.

Related *Fueling the Revenue Engine* Podcast Episode:
- Episode 7: Agile Approach to Sales Enablement

Chapter 10 Debrief:

Consider the following scenarios:
- When have you been part of a training that was well run, but you ultimately didn't adopt the skills fully because the follow-up was not well structured or was missing entirely from the program?
- What challenges do you anticipate running into when designing your own follow-up to anchor your programs?
- How do you plan to induce stakeholders and learners to invest in different forms of follow-up after the initial training?

Applied Learning:

Think of an upcoming program you need to design:
- Create a draft plan of 2 types of options for Phase 1, pre-work.
- Create a draft plan of 2 types of options for Phase 3, follow-up.

PART TWO: A Closer Look at Enablement Projects

Welcome to Part Two. Now that we've established our best practices for designing training—exploring both the how and the why of their efficacy—let's dive into the typical enablement projects and programs you will encounter. We invite you to read these chapters in the order that most supports your current priorities.

We'll unpack the details in the following chapters:

Typical Projects and Programs

- **Chapter 11:** GTM New Hire Onboarding
- **Chapter 12:** 30/60/90-Day Plans for GTM New Hire Onboarding
- **Chapter 13:** Sales/Success Process
- **Chapter 14:** Product Training and Resources
- **Chapter 15:** Competitive Intelligence and Deep Dives
- **Chapter 16:** Revenue Generating Skills
- **Chapter 17:** Coaching and Mentoring
- **Chapter 18:** GTM Kickoff, Midyear Kickoff, and Quarterly Business Reviews
- **Chapter 19:** Resource Development
- **Chapter 20:** Technology Systems and Tools

Our hope is that you will return to these chapters as needed throughout your enablement career.

Chapter 11:
GTM New Hire Onboarding

Hiring and adding more headcount to an organization's selling roles is one of the primary ways to address the market for a service or product. If a company chooses to make no other investment in its revenue generating team besides growing it, it's still making a significant choice. Therefore, one of the most essential programs growing companies tend to focus on is role-based onboarding programs that ramp a growing team of customer-facing reps into productivity.

Planning GTM Onboarding Trainings

As a company grows and hires people into selling and customer success roles, there needs to be a way to train them. Depending on the size and maturity of your organization, a new hire may also be welcomed by an onboarding program facilitated by the Human Resources or People Operations groups, designed to orient them to the company more broadly. Whether or not your company has a robust HR function, and even if a new hire has selling experience, there are invariably nuances unique to your company's sales/success cycle, product/service, competition, customer base, pricing structures, systems and tools, etc. that need to be imparted in a role-based onboarding program.

Role-based onboarding is typically a learning path of multi-session courses that build the foundation a new hire needs to be productive in their specific role. To begin your program design, we suggest starting as you would for any training: by defining your objectives based on the knowledge, tools, and skill set you need learners to exit the program with and identifying the metrics you want to track.

Inventory of Topics

Structuring the content you need to deliver in order to achieve these objectives can feel like a significant task. We recommend that you create an inventory of topics/sessions required to meet the learning objectives relevant to the role you are training. It's also helpful to present the topics in the order of the customer journey whenever possible.

Early in the learning path, outline the tools the relevant team uses and how they use them. You want to cover the tools early on so your learner can leverage them from the start as part of their applied learning and integration into their role.

Topics to cover typically include:
- ROE for the role
- Overview of your space/industry
- Pain points or problems your product or service solves
- Buyer personas and what they care about related to your offering
- Be sure to include the practitioner/user-level persona and the strategic/management-level persona and their different motivations
- Detailed product and demo training (appropriate for the role)
- Competitive intel
- Role-specific skills
   - Prospecting for SDR/BDR/AEs
   - Selling skills, pricing, negotiations, forecasting, legal for AEs, AMs, and CSMs

▫ Customer onboarding, QBR/EBR, expansion, renewal for AEs, AMs, and CSMs

Designing Onboarding Trainings

One strategic, time-efficient way to design your onboarding training is to make use of pre-existing trainings that your company may have already developed. Compare the topics you need to cover with the existing content. How can you use an agile approach to update and build on top of what's already in place?

Whether you're able to capitalize on pre-existing material or not, as you design the onboarding program, it's critical to consider the current strategic needs of the business and prioritize your development accordingly.

Then determine the best delivery and assessment methods for each topic you identify. Good starting points to consider are:
- What will the rep have to do with this knowledge?
- Does the rep need to commit this to memory, present it to a customer, or just be aware of it at a basic level?
- What are the corresponding Bloom's levels?

By incorporating application exercises into each session, you give learners experience putting the knowledge to use, making them more likely to be able to leverage it in real time when they're working with buyers.

Best practice for application is to assign each new hire a lead or account at the beginning of their onboarding program. Give them basic information such as lead name, title, company, pain points, current solution, and competitive considerations. You may choose to use real leads/accounts or rely on hypotheticals. At the end of each session, have the new hire apply their learning to their lead/account. This method works for all different types of sessions (e.g., product, selling skills, tools training). We also recommend assigning a capstone project that asks the new hire to give a presentation that demonstrates the knowledge they've learned, as if they were presenting it to the lead/customer they've been working with throughout the program. This capstone is your way of assessing that the new hire is customer ready and can graduate from the onboarding program.

Further considerations:
- As you finalize the onboarding training design, be sure to:
- Determine the time frame for training, both start date and duration.
    - If possible, try to have cohorts of new hires go through the onboarding experience together. This makes for a more impactful learning experience, gives them a buddy from day one, and makes it easier on you to facilitate the program in a scalable way. Many companies align their new hire start dates to the same day of the month so they can run the program monthly.
- Align with stakeholders to get their buy-in, asking them to review content if needed.
- Determine the best person to deliver each session.
- In many cases, the SME or stakeholder is the best person, but you should still be prepared to introduce and manage the session.

Delivering Training

Onboarding can take many forms, depending largely on whether you're in person or virtual and whether you're training one person or a group of people. You may opt for classroom style sessions, 1:1 mentoring, or self study sessions, delivered via written material, videos, and the like.

Live classroom sessions (offered either in person or virtually) are typically used for training on curriculum and/or a specific skill set that the entire group needs to learn at the same time. Classrooms are useful for the ability to use interactive exercises, field questions, and engage in facilitated discussion around topics such as product offerings, pricing, competitive positioning, etc.

Individual mentoring is useful for ongoing development and applied learning where the learner would strongly benefit from customized knowledge delivery tailored to their personal circumstances and unique learning curve. Front-line managers and/or more tenured reps are often excellent choices to provide mentorship to new hires. Whether you or someone else is doing the mentoring, be sure to set clear guidelines regarding what needs to be accomplished in each session.

Self-paced training is a third option that provides an efficient framework to deliver content in a scalable way, especially when using a learning management system. Depending on the topic, self study can be used as the primary training modality, or it can supplement and reinforce live sessions. Self study formats are ideally suited to content that can be broken into learning modules or paths. Self study is also an effective way to offer application activities and thorough assessment exercises. Before making this decision, be sure your LMS has the capability to support your design.

Depending on the circumstances, you may choose to develop an onboarding training that makes use of all three modalities. And regardless of the delivery, you will need a set of tools. We suggest the following:

- Physical or digital participant workbooks and guides
- Instructor decks
- Facilitator guides
- Text/written content
- Video content
- Learning management systems
- Knowledge management platforms

When scheduling your training, both the individual sessions and overall program, there are some logistical factors to consider. We frequently refer to the checklist below for planning purposes.

Things to consider regarding duration of training sessions and overall program:
- How much total content do you need to deliver?
- How is the content structured?
- What mode of delivery or blend of delivery methods are you using?
- What are the other demands on the participant time and energy (other meetings, in-role activities like starting to sell or take customer-facing meetings)?

- How much can people really learn in one day before they mentally check out?
- What is the best balance of live/ live virtual sessions, self-paced work, application activity, and shadowing of peers in their role?
- When and how will participants be expected to apply the concepts in real situations before moving on to the next topic?
- Do the sessions build on each other in a specific sequence?
- How much time do you need for assessment, feedback, questions/clarification, and review?
- What are the expectations regarding time to production/quota in role?
- What is the expectation of support from the new hire's direct manager?
  - Who will review application submissions?
  - Who will ensure that the new hire completes all coursework?
  - How will overlap and competing priorities be handled as the new hire transitions from onboarding/learning content into the day-to-day demands of stepping into the role they were hired for?

Important Metrics

To evaluate the overall success of your training program, you'll want to monitor the following metrics over and beyond the course of the new hire's first 90 days. Note that monitoring the specific performance of any individual rep is not your goal here. To effectively gauge how well the program enables new hires, you'll need to look at the results of all reps who have progressed through the program in its current state.
Monitoring the effectiveness of your onboarding program (and revising it accordingly) is an ongoing pursuit. Building the program is never "done," and it should evolve based on the results of the metrics you track and the needs of the business and new hires.

1. Efficiency/Time Management
   - Time to completion of all onboarding activities

- If onboarding includes any self-paced modules, be sure to measure how long it takes the new hires to complete the program and demonstrate their knowledge.
- Time to customer-facing readiness
  - How soon are reps ready to engage with customers without the assistance of a manager or experienced team member?
- Time to first closed sale
  - How long does it take them to close their first deal?
- Time to ramp
  - How efficiently did the reps pick up the necessary skill set to reach full productivity? Which area(s) of learning (if any) took longer than expected?
- Time to meet/track to quota attainment
  - Did the reps meet (or are they tracking to hit) quota within the expected time frame? If not, why and by what margin?
- Sales cycle length
  - Are the new reps moving deals through the sales cycle at an appropriate cadence? Which stage(s) (if any) are exceeding expected days in stage?

2. Customer Readiness/Performance
   - Milestone certification scores
     - E.g., pitch, discovery, demo, pricing
   - Capstone
     - Did the reps' final project demonstrate adequate competency to consider them customer ready? What further support (if any) do they need at this time?
   - Conversion rates at various intervals (1 month vs. 3 months)
     - Are the reps' conversion rates progressing as expected between intervals? What further support (if any) do they need at this time?

Taking the time to design, deliver, and continually update effective onboarding is an investment worth making. It's a high-profile program with far reaching impacts across the revenue organization. When new hires are ramped properly, they stand to reach their full potential and the organization can expect to profit accordingly.

Related *Fueling the Revenue Engine* Podcast Episode:
- Episode 16: Optimizing Onboarding in a Hybrid World

Chapter 11 Debrief:
- What was the hardest part of the planning process?
- What did you discover that you didn't expect as you went through the planning process?
- What delivery methods do you plan to use (at least initially) for the first onboarding program? Why?
- How did the list of considerations affect your decisions regarding onboarding duration? Which considerations forced you to make changes? Why?
- Which metrics do you plan to use (at least initially) for the first onboarding program? Why?

Applied Learning:
- Utilize the planning sequence, delivery options, tools, duration considerations, and metrics information above to build out the project plan for your onboarding program.

Chapter 12:
30/60/90-Day Plans
for GTM New Hire Onboarding

To accompany the role-based onboarding program you will design, new hires often adhere to a 30/60/90-day onboarding plan. This plan reinforces the role-based onboarding while offering the new hire specific month-by-month guidelines and benchmarks. Recall that the enablement-focused 30/60/90-day plan we presented in Chapter 3 as a guide to learning your new Enablement role was organized by topic and time frame. You will now be using this same structure to create role-based 30/60/90-day plans for the selling teams. And please note: It's best practice for the new hire's manager to collaborate with Enablement to build these plans.

30/60/90-day plans provide a point of reference to the new hire, helping them determine where they should focus in order to meet the needs and expectations of their role. Both new reps and their managers find them particularly helpful to navigate the ramp phase for goal-oriented roles, especially if they're using on target earnings (OTE) plans. FLMs can also use these plans to anchor their 1:1 meetings with the new hire, as well as gauge the new hire's level of initiative and self-starter mentality.

Month over month, the onboarding plan should build in complexity, learning, and proficiency. We advise that the first

30 days be dedicated to learning, followed by a focus on practice and application in months two and three. Breaking the plan into Goals, Process, Products, Tools, and Industry with monthly checkpoints will help to streamline your efforts. By the end of 90 days, a new hire should emerge with the ability to apply the knowledge and skills needed to succeed.

The progression delineated below is most applicable to an Account Executive new hire. Other GTM roles will have different expectations, but you can use the same groupings/categories.

First 30 Days: Learning

The first 30 days on the job for any role are all about learning. You can aid the learning curve by building a foundational program for these first 30 days that orients the new hire to the key responsibilities of their role. Depending on the size and scope of your organization, there will be some variety in the goals and expectations, but generally speaking, the first month is a time to build foundational skills, become familiar with the revenue organization's systems and software, and review prospective and/or customer accounts. During this time, new hires should also conduct their first mock pitches with managers, mentors, and peers. By day 30, expect your new hire to earn both pitch and capstone certifications, as well as achieve proficiency in delivering at least five customer stories, preferably in a mix of verticals. More holistically, at the end of 30 days, new hires should understand how and why your products and/or services differentiate your company within your industry.

To help new hires achieve these goals, facilitate an overview of your organization's sales process within the first 30 days. This window of time is the new hire's optimum opportunity to learn the methodology and operational sales process the sales team adheres to, as well as develop an understanding of your organization's industry, product, and customers. Best practices include having them read sales playbooks, review case studies, and practice the current presentation decks. Be sure that each new hire sets up 1:1 time with their manager to set clear goals. Coordinate shadowing sessions with their peers to learn best practices, focusing on basics to start. If you have call coaching technology like Gong or Chorus, another way for reps to learn from peers is to listen to assigned calls from a curated library of examples. New hires should be learning the relevant pitches and related talking points, becoming aware of the common objections and qualifying questions they're likely to encounter, and adopting best practices for calls and emails. Another way to bolster their knowledge is to suggest that they join industry related groups on LinkedIn. The first 30 days are also an opportune time for them to start building territory and account plans.

The table below offers some typical benchmarks for the first 30 days in a new Sales role. Please note that this is not a hard and fast rubric; you will need to customize these learning goals to fit the unique needs of your organization.

First 60 Days: Practice

As with the guidance on the first 30 days above, depending on the particulars of your company, there is variability in what

Figure 12.1: Sample benchmarks for the first 30 days: learning

Goals
- Complete onboarding bootcamp
- Conduct mock pitches (2 with managers and mentor)
- Review prospect accounts
- Be familiar with how to use the CRM to manage accounts and opportunities
- Pass pitch and capstone certifications
- Be proficient in delivering at least 5 customer stories (mix of verticals where applicable)

Process
- Review sales process
- Learn company sales methodology
- Read sales playbooks to understand sales process and activities
- Have 1:1 with your manager to set clear goals
- Shadow peers to learn best practices, focusing on basics to start
- Be aware of the common objections and qualifying questions
- Build territory and account plan

Products
- Learn about the product and customers
- Review the elevator pitch and related talking points
- Learn email and call best practices
- Review and practice the current sales pitch and decks

Tools
- Learn the tools used by your team and how they use them

Industry
- Understand the basic concepts of the things you are selling
- Understand the basic concepts of the industry you're selling to
- Understand why your products and/or services differentiate your company
- Review customer case studies
- Join industry-related groups on LinkedIn

goals are appropriate to expect during month two. The overall focus is on putting the learning into action. During this time you can expect the new hire to deepen their understanding of your product's details and your organization's culture. Encourage them to spend time with peers to learn the advanced "tricks of the trade." It's also a good time for the new hire to familiarize themselves with the major industry players on both the seller and buyer sides.

If a new hire is successfully practicing what they've learned thus far, an ideal goal for the first 60 days is to have their first "win," which could be a closed won deal or being on track toward it, depending on the sales cycle of your organization. In service of that "win," ensure that the new hire is creating at least one detailed close plan with a prospective customer that identifies how both parties will work toward completing the deal by a certain date. If you have a complex sales cycle that is significantly longer, you can substitute another measure of meaningful deal development in place of a closed won deal.

Other outcomes of continued practice include expecting the new hire to have reached their one-month ramp attainment, i.e., hitting their on target earnings (OTE), activity and revenue goals that are prorated for their ramp period. Having hit that target, we typically advise GTM Enablement teams to push new hires toward 2x pipe coverage in their second month. Like all goals, this varies based on the organization, but cultivating twice as many leads as the number of deals they need to close is generally an appropriate ratio to aim for by the end of 60 days.

You can also expect a new hire to have gained a more detailed understanding of the product they are selling/supporting as a result of their practiced efforts. A typical goal within the first 60 days is for them to earn product certification and to have conducted ten early-stage calls with prospective accounts, either self-sourced or from an account list. These introductory or "first" calls are an excellent way for them to practice articulating the details and the value of the product, learn to confidently deliver the sales pitch with different buyer personas and industries, and master the art of giving an overview product demo.

Although they have gained much proficiency, the new hire is still relatively new to the organization. While they may be well versed on pricing and discounting policies by this time, we recommend that they continue reviewing customer account plans and confirming all pricing with their manager before engaging in customer-facing pricing calls.

In addition to practice-based learning, the second month is also an opportunity for the new hire to dive deeper into your organization's day-to-day operations and process. They should be having 1:1 meetings with their manager for pipeline management and coaching, strengthening their understanding of how to recognize a real opportunity, how to drive the sales cycle, and how to work effectively with partners. In the second month, you can encourage them to focus on the more advanced activities of the sales process, such as conducting a trial or coordinating with the technical sales team on advanced use case validation or integrations.

We elaborate below on some industry standard practice-oriented goals for the first 60 days, and we encourage you to modify these as best suits your organization.

Figure 12.2: Sample benchmarks for the first 60 days: learning

Goals
- FIRST WIN
- Create 1 detailed close plan with prospect
- 1-month ramp attainment
- 2x pipe coverage for next month
- Product certification
- Conduct 10 initial/first calls
- Review customer account plans with manager
- Review pricing with manager before each pricing call

Process
- Have 1:1 with manager for pipeline management and coaching
- Understand how to drive the sales cycle
- Learn how to work with partners
- Know how to recognize a real opportunity
- Focus on the more advanced activities of the sales process, such as conducting a trial

Products
- Master the sales pitch with different personas and industries
- Be confident in pricing and discounting policies
- Master giving an overview demo
- Learn additional details about the product and organization

Tools
- Learn advanced "tricks of the trade" from peers on the tools they use often

Industry
- Become familiar with the major industry players (on both the seller and buyer sides)

First 90 Days: Application

The third month in a role is when the not-so-new hire should begin synthesizing what they've learned and practiced over their first two months and start applying their training to more and more aspects of the job.

Typically, goals by day 90 include two-month ramp attainment (if following an OTE plan) and cultivating 3x pipeline coverage for the next three months. This is a very common requirement for ongoing pipeline coverage. Depending on conversion rates, coverage at this level generally provides an adequate number of opportunities to be able to achieve revenue targets. The third month is also a good time for the new hire to complete a professional development plan with their manager, setting goals for the next quarter. By the third month, we typically see new hires creating at least two outbound campaigns prospecting for new business, as well as mastering the CRM, keeping all account records organized and up to date. This is also a good opportunity to have a new hire present as an expert in team meetings on a topic they have been learning about in their onboarding. Depending on industry, segment, deal size, and sales cycle length, it may also be appropriate for a new hire to complete at least one of each deal type: trial, master services agreement, partnership, and expansion.

By day 90, the new hire's work process should typically include 1:1 meetings with their manager for deal-level and skills-focused coaching. At this point, they should be well versed in how your company negotiates, as well as how to spot red flags during a sale. They should also understand your company's forecast, how to manage it, and how to report it. In addition, by day 90 you'll want them to be able to coordinate with technology partners and/or service providers to augment their territory plan.

You can expect the new hire's understanding of your company's product(s) to deepen even further during the third month. They should be learning the appropriate add-on services/products, when to position them, and how to demo them. On a related note, they should also be comfortable customizing the technology available to them to optimize their work performance. Another way they can become a more effective team member in their third month is to start following and reading influential industry-related blogs and publications.

Figure 12.3: Sample benchmarks for the first 90 days: learning

Goals
- 2-month ramp attainment
- 3x pipe coverage
- Complete professional development plan with manager, setting professional development goals for the next quarter
- Create 2 outbound campaigns
- Master CRM, including notes and housekeeping
- Present as an SME in team meetings
- Complete one of each deal type: trial, MSA, partner, expansion

Process
- Have 1:1 with manager for deal-level and skills-focused coaching
- Know how your company negotiates
- Learn what the red flags are during a sale
- Understand company's forecast, how to manage it, and how to report it
- Create a plan to work with partners to augment territory plan

Products
- Learn the add-on services/products, when to position them, and how to demo them

Tools
- Customize the tools for optimum performance

Industry
- Follow and read influential industry-related blogs and publications

Chapter 12 Debrief:

- If you look at your company and offerings, are there any topics you think you should add to Process, Products, Tools, Industry, and Goals? Why?
- What are the most important things you want to make sure are included within each topic in the 30/60/90-day plan? Why?
- What do you need to consider when making different versions of the 30/60/90 plan based on role (SDR, AE, Success)?

Applied Learning:

- Review your onboarding program and objectives as the basis for creating a 30/60/90 plan.
- Identify the activities that lie outside the onboarding program that should be included in the 30/60/90 plan.
- Create a baseline 30/60/90 plan.
- Adapt the 30/60/90 plan for each role (SDR, AE, Success, etc.).

Chapter 13:
Sales/Success Process

When managing a GTM organization, whether you're forecasting, training new hires, or coaching rep performance, it's critical to have clearly defined sales and success processes that provide objective frameworks. Without clearly defined processes, you'll end up with as many different interpretations of what the selling and success motions should look like as you have people in the org. Managers and reps will be left with subjective judgements about where a deal/account is in the sales cycle or customer journey, and forecasting will become untethered from analytics.

In a SaaS world, selling and servicing a customer with a consistent, seamless flow is a competitive advantage and has become the prevailing expectation of the buyer/customer. Since there are many stakeholders involved in supporting a buyer/customer through their journey with your company, defined processes create the structure that GTM teams need to ensure proper support and engagement for everyone involved. Just as enablement evolved from Sales Enablement to GTM Enablement, many progressive companies are implementing a full customer journey that supports the easeful transition between Sales and Success via curated process(es).

Why Processes Matter

Implementing clearly defined sales/success processes offers benefits to individual reps and the organization as a whole.

For reps, working within an established structure creates consistent expectations for sellers/CSMs, managers, and customers. The rigor of this structure is underpinned by efficacy: prescribed activities that create a seamless customer experience result in higher conversion rates, larger deals, shorter sales cycles, reduced churn, increased expansion, and regular renewals. A known process also helps guide and provide resources to reps who may be struggling with their accounts or might otherwise opt for shortcuts. It also helps new hires ramp efficiently into full productivity.

For the company, an established sales/success process offers more granular insight into stage management, sales cycles, and forecasting. It provides a framework for coaching to support the selling/success motion and diagnostic tools to assess how deals flow through the pipeline, where they get stuck, and the impact of changes made at any point in the sales cycle. Processes also serve as a baseline from which to address new product and/or market opportunities.

Structuring Effective Processes

Companies often have separate processes for the sales and success motions, since they represent different parts of the customer life cycle. The Enablement team can serve as the glue between the two processes, making sure they work together to benefit the customer journey and provide a common language and flow within the organization.

Many companies have what they consider to be their "sales and/or success processes." In reality, they usually have a list of activities for a rep to engage in while trying to close a deal or manage a customer. The problem is that these lists usually don't map to actual seller or buyer stages, nor do they provide the guidelines needed to stage manage or move the deal/account forward. A true process should mirror the distinct stages our buyers/customers go through and clearly outline activities that build value and next action steps. When we can provide this type of process, our GTM teams will be more effective.

Establishing an effective process starts with conceptualizing the actions, documenting them, and then presenting them in a way that is easy for others to use. A process might be outlined in a spreadsheet or slide format and should be integrated to varying degrees within the CRM system that reps use to manage sales opportunities. Wherever the details of your process are held, they need to be easily accessible, referenceable, and applicable to the daily operations of the sales or success teams.

The actual build of the sales/success process is typically led, managed, and facilitated by Enablement. This effort requires collaboration between stakeholders from Enablement, Sales and Success Management, Sales Operations, Marketing, Legal, and Finance. Input from senior reps is also important to validate the approach outlined by leadership. Once the process has been built, Enablement will lead the rollout effort and training program(s) for the GTM teams.

Most sales processes have five stages, sometimes six, depending on how complex their initial qualification is and how they break up the pass from the lead generation and SDR type roles to the AE role.

Typical stages in the buyer journey as they engage in the sales process include:

Figure 13.1: Typical stages in the buyer journey

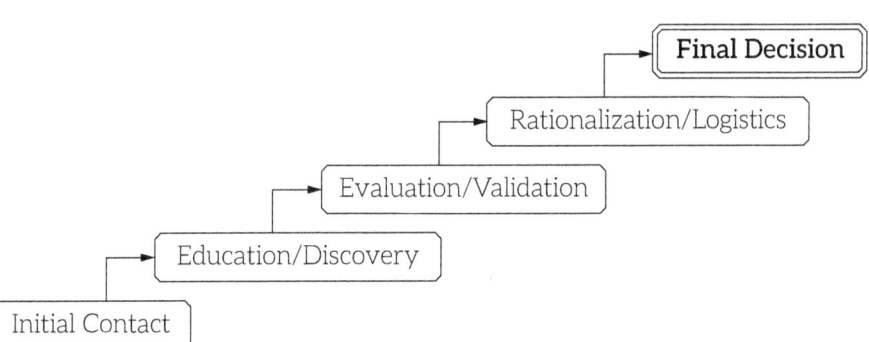

Most success processes mirror the post-sale customer journey, comprising four to five stages that focus on validating current and potential future engagement as the basis for renewal and expansion.

A typical success motion follows this rough framework:

Figure 13.2: A typical success motion

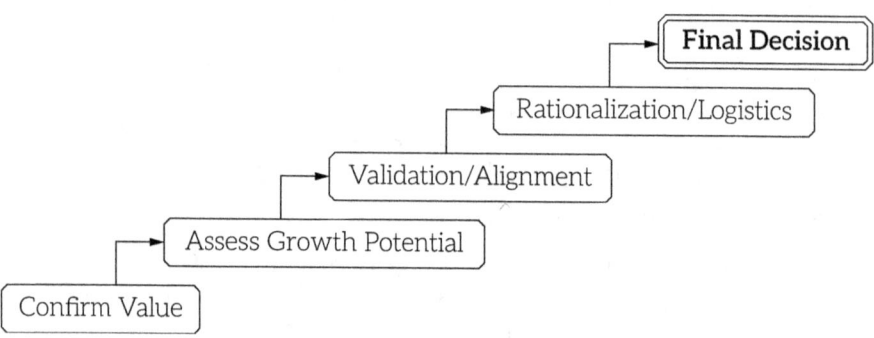

In either case, in terms of naming a stage, it's helpful to refer to the list of typical stages above. The stage name should be a label for the behavior of the buyer or customer during that stage, not what we as sellers are doing. If there are specialized terms used within your company or industry, go ahead and use them, but be careful not to fall back into a selling activity orientation while losing sight of what the buyer/customer is doing.

When building sales or success processes, the following components are important to identify and support within each stage:

- Stage number and name
- Objective of the stage (i.e., purpose and desired outcome)
- Activities to aid in forward movement of the deal
- Customer's stakeholders
- Internal stakeholders
- Resources to leverage
- Questions to ask the customer
- Questions to ask internally
- Average number of days in the stage
- Exit criteria

For each element of a given stage, you can best support your reps by first assessing:

Number and name: Consider what the buyer is doing in this stage and align the stage name with their behavior (e.g., validation). This shifts the focus to the customer and ensures that your process remains buyer centric.

Objective: What is the purpose and/or desired outcome of this stage? For example, "Initiate contact and validate mutual desire to move forward into an evaluation process that is tied to a business initiative" is a clearly defined Stage 1 objective.

Activities: What are the specific actions a rep needs to take to further qualify, build value, and/or move the deal/account along in the sales process? For example, "Confirm customer evaluation/decision-making process, people, and timeline" could be one of several critical activities in Stage 2 of a sales process.

Customer's stakeholders: Who are the key players and influencers within the customer's organization? It's critical that a rep be in conversation with the right people to ensure buy-in and alignment at each stage. For example, if it's a technical sale, both the business/financial and the technical/user stakeholders should be involved. If there are any security, finance, or legal requirements or evaluations, these stakeholders often come into play in Stages 3 and 4.

Internal stakeholders: Are there internal players the rep needs to call in? Depending on how complex your product or service is, this may be necessary. For example, a sales engineer or an executive sponsor is sometimes useful during the latter half of the sales process to answer questions, add expertise, build further rapport, validate approach, etc.

Resources to leverage: Which assets—case studies, educational videos, mutual close plans, etc.—could you supply to help move a sale/account along? Limit the scope of resources you consider to approved customer-facing resources.

Questions to ask the customer: There is, of course, no comprehensive or exhaustive list of all the questions a rep could ask during a sales cycle. Instead, give selected examples of "go to" questions that encourage your reps to lean into ongoing discovery and validation appropriate to that stage. Things like inquiring about how they can help qualify, clarify, build value, and/or create transfer of ownership are good categories of questions. An example of a customer-facing question listed in your process could be "How do you see this product solving your specific challenges?" Questions like this ask the customer to articulate an outcome and start to transfer ownership.

Questions to ask internally: The rep may also have internal questions or details they need to confirm, either with themselves or with their manager, at different stages of the deal. The purpose of these internal questions is to ensure that they have a healthy deal and are focused on the right activities in each stage that will meet the exit criteria. Examples include "Do you have contact with all identified stakeholders?" and "Does this customer have a problem that we are the best solution for?"

Average number of days in the stage: How long should this deal or account stay in a given stage? Based on the specifics of your company's product/service, your sales/success process will indicate an average number of days for a specific stage. While every deal is different and durations can vary, having realistic estimates of days in the stage will help identify if a deal is slipping or if it's stuck in a certain stage, allowing managers to diagnose and coach.

Exit criteria: What criteria must be satisfied before the deal can move to the next stage? The exit criteria are proof points that something either did or did not happen, indicating that a deal should remain in a given stage or move ahead. For example, one of the exit criteria to move a deal from Stage 1 to Stage 2 could be "Meeting has been scheduled with all identified stakeholders. Calendar invite has been sent and the meeting logged in the CRM."

All the information contained within the process serves as a guide to facilitate moving a deal/account from the initial to the final stage. Although the process is defined by stages, sometimes a certain activity, question, or resource from a later stage is useful in an earlier stage. Utilizing stage elements out of sequence is fine, but doing so doesn't mean the deal has jumped from its current stage to a subsequent one. For example, if you know the customer's procurement process is lengthy, it might make sense to start it earlier than you would for a typical sale. Starting it in Stage 3 instead of Stage 4 does not mean you have advanced your deal to Stage 4; it simply means you are utilizing a Stage 4 activity within Stage 3.

To move a deal to the next stage, meeting the current stage's exit criteria is a standard requirement. The other components of a given stage (activities, questions, etc.) exist to help move the deal forward, so they should be designed in such a way that the rep can easily leverage them as needed. Think of them as guidelines, whereas exit criteria are required. Some companies opt to create required fields in their CRM to prevent a deal from prematurely or mistakenly being moved into the next stage before the exit criteria are satisfied. Such requirements can be helpful to prevent skipping steps in the process, which will often derail a deal, causing the rep to lose control of the sale and the deal to become lost.

Many companies think they need to have different sales/success processes for different markets (e.g., small business vs. enterprise level). Best practice is to use the same process across the entire business and then consider activities to add or subtract for different markets or product lines. Similarly, a complex enterprise level sale will have more stakeholders on the customer side and/or additional days in the stage than a more transactional sale to a smaller customer. Regardless of market segment, a given deal/account must travel through the same designated stages. It's not the process but the details, complexity, and/or time within the stages that may differ.

Related *Next Level Thoughts* Blog Entry:
- Broken or Just Missing Some Pieces? Diagnosing Sales Process Shortcomings

Chapter 13 Debrief:
- Does your company have a defined sales/success process, and does it mirror the buying process/customer journey or is it more of a selling checklist broken into stages?
- Is there systems support for the current process?
- Which of the sales/success process benefits to the reps are most relevant at your company? Why?
- Which of the sales/success process benefits to the company are most relevant at your company? Why?

Applied Learning:
- Identify the internal stakeholders that hold critical knowledge and influence that you will need to build out an updated sales/success process.
- Using the current process that has been documented (if any), take a first pass at mapping the information to stages that mirror the buyer journey.
- Depending on how much information your company already has documented, you will end with the initial framework for a new sales/success process.
- Create an initial inventory of the pieces you think are missing, sorted by stage, and then stop. You cannot create a sales/success process in a vacuum without input from your stakeholders.

Chapter 14:
Product Training and Resources

Sales and Success team members need varying degrees of knowledge related to positioning and selling the products they represent. GTM Enablement works with Product Managers (PMs) and Product Marketing Managers (PMMs) as the primary SMEs within the business to train and provide resources to the selling teams for product launches and product updates. You will most likely need to deliver product training to accompany all new product launches. For product updates, the level of training or communication to the teams will depend on the complexity of the product update/release. It's helpful to partner with your PM and PMM to determine the release tier, which will determine the level of training or resources needed to enable the customer-facing teams in their selling and support efforts. Figure 14.1 provides guidelines on what to prepare for each tier.

Your job is to partner with SMEs to design and deliver the training and resources to the Sales and Success teams. In most cases product training should be delivered with the PM and PMM owners. In terms of timing, it's important to know the planned beta customer trials, product launch/product release (PR), and general availability (GA) dates, which will dictate when you schedule the training. If possible, deliver the training

Figure 14.1: Resources needed for varying tiers of product release

Tier 1: Product Launches	<ul><li>Internal launch and training</li><li>Messaging copy for Sales and Success</li><li>Customer-facing product one-pager</li><li>Product slides in first call deck/QBR deck</li><li>Internal knowledge/wiki updates</li><li>Beta customer stories and use cases</li></ul>
Tier 2: Feature Launches	<ul><li>Feature training</li><li>Messaging copy for Sales and Success</li><li>Customer-facing one-pager</li><li>Product slides for first call deck/QBR Deck</li><li>Internal knowledge/wiki updates</li><li>Beta customer stories and use cases</li></ul>
Tier 3: Minor Updates/Bug Fixes	<ul><li>Email to Sales and Success about the update/fix</li><li>Messaging copy for Success</li><li>Internal knowledge/wiki updates</li></ul>

a few weeks prior to the GA date. This schedule allows enough time for the teams to practice their pitch and demo before needing to have live conversations with customers and potential buyers.

The level of detail and timing of the training tends to differ by role. For instance, SDRs and AEs who will be selling to new customers should be trained at least one week before PR or GA dates, possibly earlier depending on the tier and complexity of the release. SEs and CSMs, however, often support beta customers, so they need to be trained further in advance and with a deeper level of technical knowledge. You may opt to train the subset of the SEs and CSMs who will be supporting the beta customers first, and then train the rest of the team as you get closer to GA. The technical Support team should be trained on how to troubleshoot the product a few weeks prior to the release, as they will be responsible to support the product at GA. In some companies, the PM will act in a support capacity for beta customers and then turn that responsibility over to the actual Support team at GA.

Topics of the training also vary by role, but the entire team needs some shared knowledge. To reference Bloom's Taxonomy, everyone on the team must be trained at the Remember and Understand levels. All team members must be able to:

- Define the new product/feature
- Recall why this product/feature is being launched
- What gaps/pains in the market dictated the decision to launch
- Articulate the value to the buyers by persona
- Why they should care about the launch
- How to message the new product features to each persona
- Show features and functionalities of the product tied back to the value
- Training should include a demo of the new product/features conducted by the PM or SE
- Reference use cases
- Retell beta customer examples and stories
- Articulate competitive differentiation
- Who else offers a similar feature
- How you do it better

Additional specific objectives dictated by role are as follows:
- AEs must be able to:
- Price the product/service
- Conduct a high-level demo
- SE/CSMs must be able to:
- Conduct a deep technical demo
- Configure the product
- Train customers on using the new product
- Support must be able to:
- Troubleshoot issues
- Configure the product

No matter whom you are training, your most important goal is to articulate the value of the new product/feature. As we explored in Chapter 2, according to Forrester, "inability to articulate value" is the number one reason why reps don't achieve quota. A strong GTM enablement program can prevent that outcome by providing the context, tools, and resources that reps need to build a consistent value proposition that resonates with potential customers.

After the training, your teams should practice their new pitch, value messaging, and demo so they'll be ready to sell once the GA or PR announcement is made. For major product launches, we recommend that you certify all reps on the new product messaging pitch and demo.

Related *Fueling the Revenue Engine* Podcast Episode:
- Episode 9: Strong Sales Enablement and Product Marketing Partnerships

Chapter 14 Debrief:
- How much interaction have you had with your Product Managers and Product Marketing Managers?
- How do you plan to set expectations about your GTM Enablement role and enroll PM/PMM in partnering with you to create meaningful training content for product training?
- How do you plan to set expectations with the Sales and Success teams regarding practice between the training and the GA dates?

Applied Learning:
- Meet with PM/PMM to determine the timelines for planned Tier 1, 2, and 3 launches and updates.
- Based on those timelines, create a tentative training schedule using the guidelines from this chapter.
- Are there any potential conflicts with things like end of quarter, end of year, or other competing priorities within the business?
- Are there any events already planned, such as SKO, that you can leverage to tie in and schedule training sessions?
- Using the training topics listed above, create templates for each role to collect the raw content/data that you will use to prepare for various product trainings.

Chapter 15: Competitive Intelligence and Deep Dives

Nearly every industry changes as new competitors enter the market and innovation creates new offerings from existing competitors. In the technology space, we see companies evolving at an especially rapid pace. But regardless of industry, all Sales and Success teams must possess the most current competitive intelligence required to position and defend their products and services against threats. Product Marketing should keep a close eye on the competitive landscape at all times and partner with GTM Enablement to keep the revenue teams trained and informed.

Not only does the competitive landscape change frequently, but your own position in the market will also shift based on your product releases and updates. In general, your releases and updates will improve your competitive position, whereas when your competitors release products or updates, you'll typically shift to defending your position. Additionally, as your product/service offerings expand, you'll almost invariably confront new competitors.

It's best practice to keep your customer-facing teams briefed on top competitors. You can do this by hosting regular competitive deep dive trainings that rotate through your list of top competitors. Doing so allows you to focus on one competitor at a time and ensures that your team takes a comprehensive look at each competitor on a regular basis. Depending on how many top competitors you face and how dynamic the market is, you may provide a competitive deep dive training once a quarter or even once a month for one of your main competitors. You can often pull data from your CRM to determine which competitors are most important to focus on.

As you prepare to design a competitive deep dive training, the most important data to focus on is as follows:
- Revenue for deals in pipeline that are at risk, going head to head with a competitor, sorted by competitor
- Revenue for deals that will require competitor to be unseated, sorted by competitor
- Revenue lost to a competitor in the last 12 months
- Revenue won against a competitor in the last 12 months

Topics to cover:
- Overview for the competitor
- What they are known for and how they position themselves in the market
- Their top features
- Traps they can set for you and how to overcome
- How you position against the competitor and how you do things better than them
- Landmines and traps you can set against the competitor
- Recent wins against the competitor, including details on how you won
- Recent losses against the competitor, including details on why you lost

There will also be smaller competitors that show up in some deals. It's very difficult to keep up with all substantive updates for every single competitor you'll face. For the competitors that show up in less than 10% of deals or don't pose a major threat, you should provide high-level positioning that can be used against any competitor included in your internal knowledge base.

Information to include in general positioning:
- Your overall product positioning
- How you do things better than the rest of the market
- Why customers choose you over other companies

Note: Competitive intel should be kept as internal facing documents and knowledge for use by your Sales and Success teams only. Making them public facing as a way of educating potential customers can backfire. If your competitive intel is made public, your competitors can easily see how you are positioned against them and you'll lose your competitive edge. Additionally, since your competitive position in the market can change frequently due to product launches and updates from either your or competitors, the intel you have put out to the public will become outdated very quickly and will harm your credibility with buyers.

Chapter 15 Debrief:
- How dynamic do you think the competitive landscape is for your products/services?
- How do you think competitive intel has helped your selling teams win deals?
- For your industry and market, what do you think are the most important aspects of competitive intel to focus on?

Applied Learning:
- Create an inventory of your top competitors.
- Using the above list of topics to include in the training, create templates for each competitor to collect raw content/data that you will use as you prepare for competitive deep dives.
- Work with Product Marketing and review CRM data to assess which competitors are most important and how often the competitive landscape shifts.
- Based on the work done above, create a competitive intel training schedule.

Chapter 16: Revenue Generating Skills

The ultimate driving force and rationale for GTM Enablement is to ensure that revenue generating teams are as productive as they can be. Revenue productivity is commonly bottom lined by measuring how many reps are consistently hitting quota. In order to achieve productivity, the team will need the selling skills and acumen to guide a buyer through their evaluation/buying process, moving deals through the pipeline as a result. These skills are just as applicable to Success team members who are directly or indirectly responsible for renewals and expansion of existing customers.

The GTM Enablement function should always be monitoring the revenue generating skills of the team to determine what skills need to be developed and reinforced. Keeping abreast of the various competencies across a team can be challenging, especially if your company is doing a lot of hiring and/or internal promotions within teams. Your revenue teams will likely have a varied range of skills, but you should strive to keep upleveling the skills of the entire team by offering skills training on a regular basis.

We have identified the following skills as essential functions that should be routinely trained/retrained:

- Pipeline management
- Account/territory management
- Prospecting/cold calling/outreach
- Qualification
- Discovery
- Relationship building
- Stakeholder mapping
- Active listening
- Communication
- Value selling/value demos
- Executive selling
- Executive QBR/EBR
- Multithreading in an organization
- Objection handling
- Negotiation
- Forecasting
- Closing techniques
- Post-sale relationship management
- Contract renewals
- Identifying and developing upsell and expansion opportunities
- Time management and tying daily activities back to quota achievement

Stay engaged with the GTM organization to determine which skills need development or refreshing. You will get clues for what to focus on by monitoring where reps are getting stuck in the sales cycle. At which stages do deals stall or take longer than expected? And where in the sales cycle are deals closed lost? By keeping abreast of how the pipeline is functioning (is the rep actively generating new business or are all leads inbounds?), you'll know which revenue generating skills to train.

You'll also learn about your teams' needs by listening in on internal QBRs, Sales/Success team meetings, and live customer calls (either live or using call coaching tools like Gong or

Chorus). Pay attention to the questions the GTM teams ask. The clarification they're seeking is a good indicator of what knowledge may need reinforcement and what existing trainings you need to adapt for the next cohort of learners. We also encourage you to meet regularly with front-line sales and success managers to understand the gaps they perceive among their teams.

Over time, you should build out resources to address the variety of skills needed by sales and success professionals. Eventually, you'll be able to draw from your inventory of trainings with minimal customization or updating. Remember to plan for reinforcement and MLOs; these follow-up activities allow for practice and keep the skills top of mind so they become habit for the GTM team. When evaluating resources to build your inventory of training content to support reps' skill development, you may have the expertise and bandwidth to build the courses in house, or you may choose to utilize a third-party skills training company to teach some or all of the skills. Many modern GTM organizations are doing a blend of both as a way to balance cost considerations with the need for outsourced expertise.

Related *Fueling the Revenue Engine* Podcast Episode:
- Episode 8: In the Trenches: AE Perspective on Enablement

Chapter 16 Debrief:
- What are your initial thoughts regarding your GTM teams' effectiveness/productivity and how skill set plays a role?
- What resources and expertise do you have available to you in house to create revenue generating skills trainings?
- What level of support do you have from the GTM leaders to prioritize revenue generating skills training? Do they see the same gaps in skill set as you do? How much work do you need to do to enroll them in the importance of this type of training?

Applied Learning:
- Using the lists above, start to audit the effectiveness of the GTM teams.
- Compare this audit to your initial thoughts in the debrief above.
- Based on your audits and the list of skills topics above, create an initial list of areas to focus on for revenue generating skills.
- Validate your skills list with GTM leaders to get their input as well as determine priorities.

Chapter 17:
Coaching and Mentoring

One of the most effective ways to reinforce training and develop talent is through coaching and mentoring programs. In addition to initial training and ongoing learning opportunities, coaching and mentoring provide customized support. When done effectively, they act as multipliers, helping individuals hone their skills and analytical capacity, making them more effective in their roles. At the management and executive levels, coaching can be seen as an insurance policy. When you think of the amount of revenue GTM leaders are responsible for and combine that with how much recruiting and retaining top management talent costs, there is a lot at stake. If a coaching program can make a leader more effective, as well as retain them in their role for a longer period of time, the return on the coaching "insurance policy" is well worth the time and resources invested.

Enablement programs that effectively reinforce learning and develop talent do so in part by providing a level of coaching and mentoring from front-line managers (FLMs), peers, and/or Enablement. To properly execute this support, the GTM Enablement team must include the infrastructure and resources for effective coaching as part of the program. For example, as part of a new sales process rollout, Enablement creates coaching guides or scoreboards to enable the FLM to effectively coach and manage to the new sales process. These coaching resources are launched to the FLM with guidance on how to use them, and they provide the FLM with the structure and resources to ask the right questions in day-to-day deal conversations with reps. Incorporating this level of structure, coaching, and enablement guidelines empowers the managers to take an active role in reinforcing the use of the new sales process.

What Is Coaching?

Coaching can be defined as the process of building the awareness, analytical capacity, decision-making, and execution skills required to achieve a desired outcome. Sales/Success coaching creates the framework to integrate training into practical application, nurture a rep's potential, and accelerate performance. Allowing for trial and error, the process of problem solving, and accountability are also important components of a coaching program.

True coaching differs from training or mentoring in that it is not a skill set transfer or a process of instructing someone on how to achieve an outcome. A coaching approach rests instead on the fundamental premise of developing the coachee's capacity to draw on their own intellect to find their own answers, design strategies, leverage resources, try different approaches, and be willing to be held accountable. Even if the coach knows the "right" answers, their job is not to tell, but instead to ask questions and offer perspective that will build awareness and analytical capacity in the person being coached, helping them arrive at their own empowered decision and path forward.

What Is Mentoring?

Mentoring is another way of supporting reps, especially if they are new hires or new to a skill or process. Mentoring provides a structure to take the experience of a more senior person in the org (sometimes a manager, but often a senior rep) and share that wisdom in service of accelerating development in others. Mentoring can include teaching, advising, sharing best practices, and giving practical advice or opinions and is usually done on a 1:1 basis.

Mentoring can also be used as support for career path development for more tenured reps. Ambitious reps can benefit from the experience of someone who has successfully developed their own sales or success career. The mentor can share their experiences, including trials and errors, as a way of positioning and accelerating the mentee's career development.

Mentoring programs can be formal or informal in nature. If there is a formal program in place, it's helpful to provide both mentors and mentees with some basic guidelines around expectations and structure so they can both benefit from the program.

Who are the best candidates for coaching?

If we go back to the premise of using coaching as a performance multiplier and insurance policy, it's important to determine the best use of coaching time and resources. If coaching or mentoring is not being made available to everyone, you need criteria to determine eligibility for the programs.

As you decide how to allocate resources for coaching reps as well as managers, consider the following:
- New hires—which of them need support to accelerate their ramp into effectiveness in their role
- High potential individuals—which of them are most primed to shift from good to great with some support, and/or which of them would benefit from support in anticipation of promotion into their next role within the org
- Top performers—which of them would be most responsive to some additional energy invested in retaining them and keeping them learning, growing, and engaged

Coaching as part of performance management:

In addition to new hires, high potential, and top performers, coaching can be an important component of performance management for reps who are underperforming. Coaching for underperformers, typically in the form of a Performance Improvement Plan (PIP), should be specific and time-bound, as coaching resources need to be balanced with the business need for using them in more effective areas as a multiplier. PIPs are often the last effort before considering reassignment or termination, but they can also create the structure and support a rep needs to achieve sustainable performance.

For a coaching effort to effectively support the PIP, the coaching must be geared toward developing analytical skill, competence, and execution toward the identified performance metrics. Initially, there will be more modeling or showing required, but over time there needs to be a transfer of responsibility for execution to the rep.

If the PIP is successful in achieving acceptable performance, continue to focus ongoing coaching on additional areas of development with the rep. Every rep has opportunities for growth, and coaching should evolve from PIP to growth coaching.

Implementing a Coaching Program

For coaching programs to be successful, you must create an environment where the programs can thrive. Prioritizing time for coaching or mentoring sessions is often a challenge, so a culture of learning and development must be supported by GTM management, not just Enablement. Coaching time can easily be eaten up by things like team meetings, deal or pipeline reviews, etc., so clear guidelines around how coaching time is to be used will be critical.

In terms of time management and scalability, there are times when 1:1 coaching is required for a specific focus with a rep, but coaching can be carried out in small groups if there is a relevant topic that applies to several team members. Technology can also help; call coaching services like Gong or Chorus offer ways to coach that leverage AI and data from real customer calls. Currently, this type of technology is among the most impactful tools in the GTM Enablement tech stack. These tools have become even more important for remote or hybrid teams where reps and managers are not typically sitting next to, learning from, or offering feedback to each other in real time, the way teams function when based in the same physical location and routinely overhearing each other's calls. Another added bonus of call coaching technology is that it takes away the need to role-play customer calls and/or have the rep recap their impression of a call; these subjective experiences are replaced with the data of what actually happened on a call, what the rep said, what the customer said, etc., which is the basis for more advanced levels of coaching. The data also provides a tremendous amount of feedback to the Enablement and GTM leadership team regarding how training is being adopted and where reinforcement, additional training, or skill development is needed.

Despite the many benefits, Enablement must ensure that the call coaching tool is properly configured to provide the most effective insights and coaching opportunities for the GTM teams. To achieve the best results, Enablement must collaborate with the management team, as well as the reps, on the most effective use of this technology and data. This dynamic should be seen as an iterative process that gets honed over time.

Technology assisted or not, the FLMs are often best positioned to do the coaching. They hold the expertise around the people on their teams and the business context. Using managers as resident coaches, however, comes with some inherent challenges.

When using managers as coaches, consider:
- What training have you given the managers on how to coach vs. tell, show, or mentor?
- It's unfair to expect managers to know how to provide coaching if you haven't provided any training on how to effectively coach.
- How have the goals of the coaching been defined and communicated?
- If there is a lack of direction here, the coaching could end up addressing things that aren't aligned with critical initiatives.
- What are the agreements around confidentiality and the content of the coaching sessions?
- People need to feel like they can speak freely within a coaching session without their challenges being discussed with others.

In some cases, bringing in an outside resource as a coach that is skilled in sales/revenue coaching is the most appropriate solution. An outside resource can alleviate many of the time and coaching skill concerns. Additionally, having someone other than a direct manager can create an environment where reps feel safer sharing and debriefing difficult calls.

Coaching program resources:

In addition to the call coaching technologies previously mentioned, there are skill tracking resources we find useful to keep a record of each rep's development. Having their progress plotted and noted in a systematic way will help you structure more comprehensive coaching conversations down the road.

If the team you're working with already has a coaching and professional development tool that has been implemented by the Human Resources/People team, you can adapt these resources to use in conjunction with that tool.

Attribute and Skill Set Matrix

An Attribute and Skill Set Matrix plots selected attributes against corresponding skill sets identified by management as priority skills to cultivate. The grid format allows you to quickly scan and verify skills that are being executed on, as well as identify areas of development. This information will inform the direction of your coaching conversations.

To implement this type of matrix; you will need to partner with your GTM leadership to determine what attributes are most critical to rep development as well as the success of the organization. Once the attributes are defined, corresponding skills should be selected under each attribute. It's helpful to build different matrices for each role you coach. Here is one example of an Attribute and Skill Set Matrix that we find helpful when coaching SDR and/or AE roles

Figure 17.1: Attribute and skill set matrix

Attribute	Skills
Execution	• Outreach process & techniques • Pipeline management • Utilizes tools & resources • Meets quota & call volume
Training & Certifications	• New hire training • Demo certification • Competitive certification • Specialty certification
Sales Acumen	• Understands qualification criteria & profile • Adept at selling to multiple stakeholders and buyer personas • Successfully converts opportunities through sales stages • Time management & organization
Professional Standards	• Independent & driven to succeed • Trustworthy & has integrity • Displays high standards of professionalism • Process improvement
Continued Development & Leadership	• Continual learning • Team focused & collaborative • Leadership opportunities • Feedback, coachability & communication
Culture Embracing	• Culture builder • Core values understanding & adoption • Enjoys coworkers—active participant in corporate activities • Cross-functional communication outside Sales

Figure 17.2: Indicator chart

Attribute	Behaviors	Positive Indicators	Needs Growth Indicators	Negative Indicators
Execution				
Training & Certifications				
Sales Acumen				
Professional Standards				
Continued Development & Leadership				
Culture Embracing				

Describe **behaviors** you are expecting to see related to the attribute

Describe the **positive indicators** related to this attribute (i.e., when you see these things, you know the rep is doing well)

Describe the indicators of **need for growth** related to this attribute (i.e., when you see these things, you know the rep is still ramping or needs additional support)

Describe **negative indicators** related to this attribute (i.e., when you see these things, they give you pause and create concern)

Indicator Chart

An Indicator Chart pairs with the Attribute and Skill Set Matrix to pinpoint which specific behaviors you're looking for in each attribute area. Indicator Charts allow you to communicate what behaviors you are looking to see as the objective measure of expected execution. They also have columns to note positive, growth, and negative indicators. Positive indicators are what you see when things are going well. Growth indicators might reveal a rep is still ramping as a new hire or that they need some additional support, training, or structure to be successful in their role. Negative indicators are the things that give you pause and create concern. Having all of these measures of performance clearly defined creates objective criteria beyond just quota to measure against and coach to.

Coaching Profile

A Coaching Profile is your tool to document personal profile information for the people you coach. These profiles are typically used by managers who coach their own team. Whether you utilize a performance management system or store this information in a standalone document, having a detailed profile of each team member's unique motivations, values, and more gives context to the coaching conversation and allows the coach to connect with the coachee on a level more meaningful than just performance metrics. Knowing someone's core values, aspirations, communication style, motivations, etc. is very helpful when engaging with them in a coaching capacity. We recommend that coaches maintain these profiles as living documents, adding to/refining them over time and co-creating them with the coachees. For the coachee, seeing themselves accurately documented and understood is a validating experience that helps them feel understood and supported, key drivers of success.

Figure 17.3: Coaching profile example

Employee Name: *Stephanie Bridges*

Career aspirations	Remain in quota-carrying role to build selling skills as mid-market AE, and then position herself for a promotion to the enterprise segment within the next 9 months.
Personal aspirations	Pursue an active lifestyle and community building through wildlife habitat and land use education.
Motivations	Collaboration/teamwork, challenging projects, ability to create impact, recognition of job well done.
Core values	Trust, excellence, family, health.
Talents, strengths, and skills	Natural team leader who can enroll others and build trust. Excellent presentation and communication skills.
Communication style	Is direct in her asks and not afraid to ask for clarification when needed. Prefers direct feedback as well.
Professional development needs	Needs more experience building executive level sales acumen (especially if she wants to work with enterprise customers) and ability to assess situations in real time.
Other insights	Is well networked with peers from past roles and can be leveraged to recruit additional reps. Also enjoys the education aspect of peer mentoring and could be used as a new hire mentor/buddy.

Development Plan

A Development Plan is an extension of a Coaching Profile and can be created manually or within a team management tool if you have one available to you. It provides a place to document short- and long-term goals as well as the actionable steps to achieve them. The items noted in the sample Development Plan below are only suggestions; we encourage you to customize your Development Plans to suit the organizational needs and/or professional development priorities of both you and your coachees.

Figure 17.4: Development plan example

Employee Name: *Stephanie Bridges*

Goals	Near term	Longer term
Results, performance, and achievements	Meet/exceed quota next 2 quarters, qualify for President's Club reward trip.	Maintain quota, build acumen and skills for possible promotion to enterprise rep role.
Initiatives to start and/or complete	Complete new demo certification and help review new customer education program.	Provide feedback on mentoring program and new hire onboarding/training.
Attitudes/behaviors to demonstrate	Patience and participation in deal debriefs.	More sophisticated relationship building and gain perspective on leadership.
Skills to learn	Multithreading and value selling.	Selling to C-suite executives and competitive positioning.
Knowledge to gain	Sales process and stage management.	Forecasting accuracy for longer sales cycles.

Actionable next steps	Description	By when?
New assignments and challenges	Complete 201-level learning path.	Within 3 months.
Meet key people, develop mentors, form new relationships	Shadow select reps. Meet with Enablement to assess where you can add value.	Over the next 6 months.
Get feedback and advice	Meet with top performing reps, learn best practices, set development benchmarks.	Over the next 6 months.
Attend formal training programs or conferences	Continue learning sales process, C-suite selling, and competitive positioning.	Over the next 6 months.
Join new organizations/networks	Research and join industry organizations and forums with our buyer personas.	Within 1 month.
Read and conduct self-study	Study industry trends, market landscape, and feedback from our buyers.	Ongoing.
Coaching	Continue with 1:1 coaching, add peer coaching with teammates.	Ongoing.
Other	Identify 2 other ideas to support your development.	By our next coaching meeting.

Related *Fueling the Revenue Engine* Podcast Episode:
- Episode 18: Enablement Guide to Sales Coaching

Chapter 17 Debrief:
- What experiences have you had with coaching or being coached?
- What did you like about them?
- What didn't you like?
- What would you change or add if you could go back and do it again?
- What experiences have you had with mentoring or being mentored?
- What did you like about them?
- What didn't you like?
- What would you change or add if you could go back and do it again?

Applied Learning:
- Does your company have a coaching and/or mentoring program?
- If so, is it effective? Does it need to be refreshed?
- If not, is this something you think should be implemented, and what would be the biggest benefits?
- Do you have access to call coaching technology?
- If so, take a first pass at optimizing it so it saves time and provides the most important insights.
- Double-check with Sales and Success management, as well as selected reps, to ensure they can get the benefits of it as well, adjusting as needed.
- If you plan to use front-line managers as coaches, what level of training have they had?
- Do these guidelines and trainings need to be revisited?
- Meet with your sales and success leaders to discuss and come up with a plan to implement any relevant program changes.

Chapter 18:
GTM Kickoff, Midyear Kickoff, and Quarterly Business Reviews

Kicking off the new fiscal year is always a big transition point in the year. What used to be just "Sales Kickoff" or "SKO" has grown to be more inclusive of the broader GTM team and typically includes Pre- and Post-Sales and Marketing, as well as some technical roles related to sales and implementation. Sales Kickoffs that have evolved into this larger type of event have often been re-named GTM Kickoff (GTM KO) or Revenue Kickoff (RKO) and are typically the biggest investment an organization will make on the internal team all year.

GTM KO brings remote teams together to build skills but also provides an opportunity to celebrate hard work and achievements. Even if you don't have remote teams, getting out of the usual routine of work in the office sets the stage for deeper collaboration and team building. GTM KO is a very high-profile event, often occurring over several days, and the Enablement function is usually responsible for coordinating its entirety, from the overall theme to the smallest logistics and details.

While in-person GTM KO has been and continues to be industry standard, the arrival of the global Covid pandemic in 2020 forced companies to rethink in-person events and offer remote versions instead. Even though there are aspects of in-person events that are lost in their online equivalents, we've been impressed with the ways that Enablement teams were able to replicate the energy and important elements of most kickoffs in remote formats. At this moment in time, we're seeing a combination of fully in-person events, some still fully remote events, and some hybrid models of in-person events followed by remote sessions for specific purposes like team or role-based training events. The best practices that follow apply to both in-person and remote events, and there are additional thoughts specific to remote formats at the end of this chapter.

GTM KO events are a unique opportunity to:
- Advance your GTM Enablement agenda
- Level set the GTM organization
- Roll out new corporate initiatives
- Create energy to start the year off on a high note
- Celebrate successes

Planning an Impactful Kickoff

Any successful event takes time to plan, and for a high-stakes event like GTM KO that is especially true. It's best practice to give yourself a full quarter for planning and preparation work. Since most kickoffs are scheduled for early in the first quarter of the new fiscal year, it will be your primary focus during Q4 and the first part of Q1 leading up to the event. Yes, there will inevitably be some conflict between planning your GTM KO and the push to close out Q4 and year-end! Make sure all key stakeholders, especially your revenue leaders, understand that you will need their partnership to deliver an impactful, world-class, memorable kickoff for their teams. This means that you will need their help and support leading up to the kickoff event, during their busiest quarter. Make sure they understand how important their contribution is and that they are willing to prioritize assisting you as needed in the preparation for the event.

Not dissimilar to designing a training, a planning successful kickoff starts with determining objectives. Work with the senior GTM leadership to decide what you want to accomplish at this event. How do the objectives tie into the broader organizational goals for the year? This clarity will ensure that the agenda supports those goals and avoids overpacking the program or diluting the impact of the kickoff. It will also help enroll the GTM leadership when they can see the tie to their initiatives. The objectives become the barometer to determine what fills the time during the event. Circulate those objectives with all key stakeholders so everyone is working toward the same goals.

For in-person events, we recommend you plan for a two-and-a-half or three- day event, preferably midweek. Monday should be a travel day if you have attendees coming from out of town, and a day for local reps to take care of any customer meetings before the event starts or complete pre-work for the event. Tuesday, Wednesday, and Thursday should be dedicated to the kickoff event. Friday becomes a travel day again, and a day for attendees to catch up on matters that have had to wait while they were offsite at the event all week.

For a remote event, you'll need to plan an agenda that accounts for video call fatigue. Sessions should be stacked no longer than four hours end to end on any given day—with a minimum of one break midway, if not two. Therefore, in order to hold attention and engagement from a remote audience, one day's worth of in-person content will need to be spread over two days with virtual events.

Best Practices

1. **Balance.** Whether in person or online, strive to create balance. The agenda should include a mix of education, celebration, fun, team building/networking, and rah-rah-rah. And be sure to allow downtime for the reps to catch up on important customer follow-up or just to decompress. Balance is critical to the success of the event. Without it, you'll end up with participants who are stressed, bored, and/or creating their own ways to attend to outside needs.

2. **Focus.** For the training/education portion, pick one main topic or initiative and stick with it. As with the other trainings you design, be mindful of your objectives and careful not to cram in too much! For example, are you rolling out a new product you want all the teams positioned to sell? Make that the focus of your agenda, with the end result being that every person on the team is certified to position and sell the new product.
3. **Participation.** Sessions should be interactive and activity based. Limit talk-at-you sessions. Participants don't successfully absorb information this way. As we discussed in Chapter 5, Adult Learning Theory tells us that people demonstrate the highest retention of learning when they've been taught in interactive, scenario-based learning environments. Where applicable, structure the activities with mixed-role groups so people can build relationships with coworkers they don't interact with on a daily basis and access varied perspectives on the topic at hand.
4. **Timing.** While designing the interactive sessions, allot more time than you think you will need. Time goes much faster than you expect, whether in a live or live virtual environment. Be sure to structure your program accordingly so you aren't forced to rush through other important topics due to time constraints.
5. **Relevance.** Ensure that the content of the sessions is relevant to everyone in the audience. If the event includes the entire GTM team, that means you need to consider a much broader audience than just AEs. If you are taking people away from their day job for two or three days (whether in person or remote), you need to ensure that each one of them gets something of value from it. To that end, you need to account for each role attending the session and tailor the content accordingly. Within the facilitation, you may need to give multiple examples that support the content and make sense in the context of different roles. For instance, you might present content from the Sales interpretation and then offer up the modified application for a Success role. Delivering a meaningful experience to each attendee usually requires that you offer breakout sessions by functional team or role; doing so makes the content relevant, leading to

greater rates of retention and application in each person's daily job processes.

6. **Customer Perspectives**. Invite customers to speak to your teams as part of the agenda. You can't replicate the experience from the customer perspective with role-plays or scenarios, so it's worth the effort to get customers to speak. Invitations should go out early enough to be able to get on customers' calendars, and time expectations should be clear so they aren't giving up too much time. Once you get attendees confirmed, make sure there is a clear agenda and some scripted questions to guide the panel. Questions around use cases, customer experience, why they chose you, things they value, and things they have run into problems with are great starting points. The primary GTM leader is a good choice for panel moderator. Although there are lots of considerations and coordination, customer panels are continually the highest-rated sessions by all audiences.

7. **Wins and Losses.** Other sessions that are very impactful include customer success stories and win/loss reviews. There is value in seeing all the steps in a process and debriefing successes as well as losses. It is not often that we allocate the time to take a comprehensive look at the factors that contributed to the outcomes, what we did well, what we could do better, and how our customers are using our solution successfully. This opportunity to reflect and integrate important learnings is a rare break from our go-go-go and on to the next mode of operation.

8. **Outside Speakers.** Sometimes it makes sense to invite an outside speaker to offer a different perspective on a process or challenge. Outside speakers are a great way to add credibility to an important corporate initiative. If you do choose to leverage an outside speaker, choose them based on their ability to relate to your audience and bring unique value to the conversation.

9. **Rehearsal.** Rehearse with everyone who is presenting. Yes, everyone! This means anyone who will be addressing the audience, including C-level executives. Rehearsals are a crucial opportunity to work out the inevitable logistical kinks and ensure that your timeline is accurate before

going live. It also prepares everyone to be at their best when they are standing before the entire organization.

- In an ideal world, you would rehearse an in-person event in person. But given the nature of hybrid and remote work, we believe you can successfully rehearse an in-person event online. The intention for the rehearsal is to replicate the way the sessions will be delivered, and there are multiple considerations to this. Time-wise, you should allocate **twice** the expected amount of time to rehearse every session. This recommendation is based on our experience regarding how long it takes to complete a full rehearsal. During the rehearsal, you'll need to keep track of time to confirm session duration and also listen from the audience perspective to ensure that the presentation flows well and lands properly. Based on the rehearsal, presenters sometimes make changes to their talk track and may need to repeat that section to ensure that the changes flow well. Additionally, you'll need time to explain things such as audience logistics, how breakout sessions will work, and any facilitator/presenter logistics to the presenting team. This could produce additional feedback or adjustments that weren't considered before, so you'll need time to address those. Note that you do not need to allocate rehearsal time for the time intended for participants to complete the breakout exercises.
- For both in-person and remote sessions, the rehearsal should include practice using any of the technology capabilities (audio sharing, screen sharing, host settings, co-hosting, breakout rooms, polls/surveys, etc.) that the presenter will be expected to leverage for the presentation.
- If you are doing a customer panel that is conversational, a review of the questions with the customers is probably sufficient, but if they are presenting on a use case or using slides, a real rehearsal is helpful. Even if you can't get additional time on the customer's calendar, the moderator of the panel should rehearse their portions.

- If you've invited a guest speaker, they will likely not attend the rehearsal, but you should know what topics they intend to cover, how long a presentation they'll give, and any special support they'll need. Some guest speakers may give you an advance copy of their presentation, which is helpful but not required.
10. **Technical Considerations.** For all events, you must plan for proper technical support. Your entire event will be derailed if you can't access presentations, videos, music, or other required digital files. Additionally, if you are using cloud-based collaborative materials for the session content, we always recommend downloading a copy on the day of your event. Doing so provides a backup of the final version in case the cloud server goes down during your event.
11. **Celebration!** Include team building and rah-rah-rah. Celebrate the wins from the past year and recognize the top performers. Appreciation, recognition, and acknowledgment go a long way, and when people feel like their contributions are of value, they will move mountains to do the best job they can. People in quota-carrying roles also tend to be inherently competitive, and knowing that wins are celebrated in a public forum like GTM KO can breed healthy competition.
12. **Fun!** Don't forget the fun! Plan activities that are fun just for the sake of fun. The team has worked hard all year, and at kickoff they will appreciate the fun bonding time with their team members. To that end, for in-person events, throw a killer party/awards dinner. Let the team cut loose! Do it the second night, though, so the bulk of your educational objectives have already been met. Be prepared for most of the team to be "out of it" the next morning. Plan for lighter content to wrap up the event, without needing too much brain power from your audience on that last morning. For remote events, fun team building activities and award celebrations are impactful ways for remote teams to come together virtually even when in-person events are not possible. There are many options for fun activities that can be hosted/facilitated by innovative companies that specialize

in creating remote team experiences. We encourage you not to skip this part of the agenda!
- **Note:** The kickoff Enablement team should abstain or limit their alcohol intake during the event so they have the energy to keep the event running smoothly. Perhaps you can plan a fun night for the enablement team after the event wraps!

13. **Follow-up.** As discussed in Chapter 10, follow-up is key. This is true at every scale, from an "ordinary" training to a marquis event. Once kickoff is over, make all presentations and follow-up materials available as soon as possible. If you can record all the sessions and make the recordings available, that is ideal. Engage with your front-line managers to carry forward the key concepts and learnings, reinforcing the new training content delivered during the event. Similar to following up with micro learning objects, carry the post-kickoff momentum forward by creating multiple touch points to reinforce learning:
    - Incorporate kickoff content into onboarding programs moving into the new year so all new hires are up to speed on the topics covered during kickoff.
    - Work with executives to enable them to carry forward the key messages and objectives throughout the year as they issue communications and make decisions on priorities and programs.
    - Be sure to collect success stories from reps using what was taught at kickoff, then use those stories to reinforce the training.

Planning for Breaks and Food at Kickoff Events

If you don't plan properly for breaks and food, even the best content and agenda will fail. Nobody functions well when they are tired and/or hungry. Be sure to take the following guidelines into consideration when planning your timelines:
- Attention spans will wane after concentrated blocks of time, so plan to break at least once every two hours for in-person events and once an hour for remote events.
- For in-person events:

- Always have plenty of cold water and coffee available throughout the day.
- Offer meals and break snacks.
  - There is nothing worse than running out of food, so make sure you have confirmed the headcount with your catering staff.
  - Plan to offer an assortment of foods that will accommodate dietary considerations and allergies. This means clearly labeling vegetarian/vegan items, as well as labeling any potential allergens (gluten, nuts, seafood, etc.). Be sure that you have dietary-alternative meals readily available and easily accessible for those who need them.
  - To counter morning hangovers (clichéd but inevitable), offer heartier breakfast and break snacks the morning after a party evening.
  - Fresh offerings with lean proteins (including options for vegans/vegetarians) for lunch will fill people up but not bog them down for the afternoon.
  - Your afternoon break snack should be sugary to help pick back up the energy mid-afternoon—fresh fruit, candy, and sweets are good options.
- Share the event agenda with the catering staff so they can coordinate having the food set out at least 15 minutes prior to each scheduled break and meal—planning ahead in this way will prevent a hungry crowd from circling as the catering staff scrambles to set up the food.

Prior to Kickoff

You've just solved for a significant number of important logistics… but wait, there's more. Before your event can move forward, there are still some critical considerations.

For in-person events, once you choose the location, you'll want to do a site visit to familiarize yourself with the physical layout and AV setup requirements. If you're hiring an outside AV specialist for support, they should be at the site visit so you can walk through the AV-related logistics of the day.

Some additional AV tips include:

- Ask the facility about their experience with a group your size.
- Make sure you have a strong enough wifi signal that supports all attendees, presenters, and support staff logging on at the same time.
- Keep in mind that wet or windy weather can have a large impact on wifi performance.
- When in doubt, securing additional wifi hotspots or signal boosters is a good idea.
- Test (and re-test!) any music and/or live demos of a software product using the onsite network.

Whenever possible, hard wire your presentations. Despite your best efforts (see above), wifi remains unpredictable. You want to reduce the number of things that could possibly go wrong during kickoff, and hard-wired internet connections are one way to eliminate variables. If you need to use a cloud service such as Google Slides, make backups of all your decks.

Another (strong) recommendation to remove variables is to use one computer, typically a company loaner, to run the entire program. Plan to compile all presentations for each day into a single deck, and be sure to download any necessary applications onto that computer ahead of time. Doing so ensures you have all content ready to go, allowing for seamless transitions between presenters. Letting different speakers use their own machines to give their presentations only complicates your logistics and introduces unnecessary risks.

If your kickoff needs sound amplification (depending on the size of the crowd), test the microphones you'll use for the presenters and any handheld microphones for Q&A and panels. If you choose to use mic packs for your speakers instead of a handheld microphone, be sure you have several of them, as taking a pack off of one speaker and then connecting it to the next is cumbersome and time-consuming. You'll want to be sure that a speaker waiting to speak is already mic'd while waiting for the current speaker to conclude. For speakers delivering just one relatively brief presentation, we find that handheld mics are an easier choice. Whatever you choose, be sure to rehearse. As a final word of caution about mic packs, when a speaker comes offstage, designate one person to ensure that the mic is no longer live. This prevents side conversations from being broadcasted to your entire audience.

As with all trainings you plan, do your best to record all content for future use.

Special Considerations for Remote Kickoff Events

Remote events have an additional set of technical considerations to account for, and none more so than your annual kickoff. In addition to the advice covered above, best practice for a remote kickoff is to have event production support standing by to step in and help any presenter or attendee who has technical issues. This helps guard against sessions being derailed by unexpected issues that can arise with connecting to technology or accessing presentations, video, music, or other required digital files. Additionally, you'll want to appoint support staff familiar with the content to track chat submissions and/or circle through virtual breakout rooms. Granular logistics like this play a major role in the success of remote kickoff events, since you are not in the same physical space and there's less flexibility to skillfully improvise if something goes wrong. For instance, you need to be sure that the right people get assigned to the right breakout rooms. And you need to delegate "small" tasks to your team, such as moving participants in and out of the breakout rooms, moderating each room, ensuring that someone stays in the main room, etc. You also need to decide who will be responsible for screen sharing, who will control advancing slides, and who will build out deck animations. The skillful execution of each of these details directly impacts the success of your kickoff. The only way to ensure skillful execution is practice.

One of the most important variables to account for is the quality of your presenters' technology. Confirm well ahead of kickoff that they each have access to a sufficiently strong wifi signal in the location they will be presenting from, and that they have a reliable computer. And if they intend to make use of any special technology features in their presentation, make sure that both they and your support staff are well versed in how that technology works.

Keep in mind that staying focused at an event is more challenging for attendees when they are remote versus in person. Because you can't control their environment (i.e., their distractions), we suggest taking advantage of video call engagement technology to keep them engaged. In addition, you'll need to be thoughtful about breaks, session duration, and overall length of days. Set the schedule in with attendees' time zones in mind, and plan for realistic start/end times, as well as mealtime breaks. Some companies offer attendees an allowance to expense or order meals during the event time. If yours does, be sure to communicate the day's agenda, as well as guidelines for using this allowance, ahead of time so they can order food to arrive at the right times.

As with in-person events, plan to record all sessions. This will most likely be a standard option in the video call technology you use. If so, set it to automatically record. If not, set a reminder for yourself to press record (trust us on this one; you will have many other things on your mind and it is very easy to forget this in the moment).

Midyear Kickoffs

Many companies will also host a Midyear Kickoff (MKO) as a way of recharging the team going into the second half of the year. MKOs tend to be more lightweight events and typically only one to two days in duration, but with similar goals as a regular GTM KO. Even though MKO events are usually shorter and have a smaller budget, follow the same general guidelines as you would to produce a GTM KO. Sometimes MKOs are produced as regional events in a roadshow style to save on travel costs.

Quarterly Business Reviews

In some cases, the GTM Enablement function will also host Quarterly Business Reviews (QBRs), which can double as a one-day training event for the Sales and/or Success teams. These QBRs are typically treated more like a glorified training event. Regardless of how the event is structured, refer back to instructional design and guidelines to support proper program builds.

Related *Fueling the Revenue Engine* Podcast Episode:
- Episode 12: Rethinking SKO in a Virtual World

Chapter 18 Debrief:
- What do you need to include in your plan to communicate and enroll stakeholder participation in GTM KO planning during Q4? Hint: this needs to happen early in Q4 so you aren't negotiating for time after they have launched into year-end crunch mode.
- What have you enjoyed about different GTM KO style events you have attended in the past? How do you want to incorporate some of those elements as you plan your own GTM KO?
- Did anything occur (or fail to occur) at past GTM KO events that detracted from the experience for participants? What planning do you need to do to avoid those pitfalls?

Applied Learning:
- Sketch out a draft of a three-day GTM KO agenda that includes:
- Types of sessions
- Groups/roles to include
- Logistical consideration notes, including remote considerations (if applicable)
- Potential types of locations
- Compile a list of stakeholders you will need to work with.
- Create a planning timeline that accounts for about three months of prep work.

Chapter 19:
Resource Development

Whether it's a major initiative, training reinforcement, a customized project for a specific team, or something in between, most programs need corresponding resources that are your responsibility to develop. Common examples of such resources that we detail in this chapter are playbooks, talking points for phone calls, email templates, use cases, and case studies.

Playbooks

Playbooks compile proven strategies, content, and tools into an easy-to-follow asset. They're a codification of best practices for any given situation that you want to capture and communicate to your customer-facing teams. A playbook is often released in conjunction with comprehensive training. For growing startups, playbooks are an ideal way to document tribal knowledge and share the associated best practices with new employees, ensuring consistency in the way every member of the team operates.

A good playbook is a valuable resource that lays out the steps a rep should take in differing scenarios and in real time. As such, playbooks should be stored in your company's CRM and/or KMS to make it quick and easy for reps to find the relevant information they need to address a specific situation.

You will likely need several playbooks based on the makeup of your team and your business. Typical topics for a GTM playbook could include:

- Role specific (SDR/BDR, AE, AM, CSM, by segment)
- Transition/hand-off process to another role (SDR/BDR to AE, AE to AM or CSM)
- When to position which product (can be vertical or persona dependent)
- New product launch
- New process launch
- New hire
- Qualification
- Discovery
- Demo
- Competitive
- Pricing
- Renewal
- Retention
- Expansion/growth

A playbook can assume varied formats, so it's important for you to choose one that works best for the given topic, audience, and intended use. Possible formats include:

- Steps in your CRM guiding the reps through each step of a process
- Most helpful when you can include context around the steps to guide the rep through the playbook
- Documentation easily available in the internal content/knowledge management system
- Short audio visual media modules shared in an LMS or KMS

Most likely, some but not all of the material that will go into your playbooks already exists somewhere in your company. We recommend that you audit this material, incorporate it as appropriate into the playbooks needed in this current moment, and make the newly updated resources available to the team.

Creating a playbook:

Creating a playbook can be a significant undertaking. Before developing one, we encourage you to ensure that your effort is aligned with the larger revenue organization priorities, tied to agreed-upon initiatives, and backed by the revenue leaders.

Once you have the green light, begin as you would with other enablement initiatives by outlining your goals and objectives. Determine the stakeholders and SMEs that should contribute. This group should include a mix of GTM leadership, front-line managers, individuals who will be using the playbook, and members of supporting teams such as Marketing, Customer Success, Customer Support, and Operations.

The following variables could impact the design of your playbook, regardless of topic:
- Market segment
- Select the market segments with needs that best match your differentiators.
- Competitive differentiation
- Study your competition—which segments they concentrate on and what their strengths and weaknesses are for those segments.
- Qualification criteria for ideal prospects
- Identify buyers' roles and typical titles encountered by each seller role.
- Sales/Success process (sequence of steps and order in which roles are approached, if relevant)
- Tools for stages, roles, and segments

Note that not all of these considerations will apply to every playbook type, but familiarizing yourself with them will allow you to assess where they are applicable.

The most useful playbooks include step-by-step tactical plans for how to execute on a given process. Support the plans you've outlined by including tools and collateral such as FAQs, customer testimonials, product updates, etc. An audit of your company's existing content, tools, and processes will save you from unnecessarily duplicating efforts and allow you to identify any gaps.

Once your playbook is complete and you have secured approval from your key stakeholders, you can create and launch an implementation plan. Depending on the circumstances, you may wish to design and deliver a new playbook as part of a training session. At the very least, you'll need to distribute the playbook to relevant teams. We recommend making it accessible in digital tools such as CRM, CMS, KMS, or LMS. In order for the teams to make the best use of this new playbook, give them easy access to all the assets it contains (linked assets are especially convenient for this). To ensure use of the playbook, partner with the appropriate front-line managers. Keep in mind, though, the playbook is a guide. You want to give your reps clear instruction without straitjacketing them.

The best playbooks are living documents that are reviewed and updated often. To keep your playbooks relevant, up to date, and a valuable resource for your teams, we recommend that you set up a regular review process to update and refine the playbooks. We've found that a quarterly review process is ideal to catch any changes that have gone into effect during the previous quarter. Depending on the needs of the business, sometimes the playbooks will just need a few minor updates and sometimes the reviews will result in a complete overhaul.

Call Outlines

Call outlines are a set of talking points commonly used by reps when speaking with prospects and customers. They are very useful for anyone who lacks confidence and/or experience in making live phone calls and tends to prefer written communication such as text, chat, or email. Since calls aren't always answered, it's helpful to include pointers for voicemails to go with the call outlines.

The objective of the call outline is to provide key talking points for typical customer conversations, as well as responses to common objections. Outlines assist the rep in organizing their thoughts and responses for common customer interactions and can guide a conversation in real time if they get stuck on a call.

Call outlines are most helpful when:
- Ramping new hires

- Updating market positioning
- Introducing new products or entering new markets—which likely brings new buyer personas and/or competitors

As with playbooks, your goal with call outlines is *not* to create robots! Encourage reps to use the suggested key points, but allow them the freedom and flexibility to make them their own. This means using the outlines as a structure from which to improvise, add phrasing, and/or change language to match their style, tone, etc. A rep cannot be successful trying to sound like someone else, so encourage them to customize and then practice using their modified script. Keep in mind that your outlines exist to provide guidance and focus; the reps are the ones having the conversations and developing the relationships, so they need latitude to be themselves.

Designing call outlines:
- Identify the primary area you are focusing on (e.g., product, persona, competitor).
- Develop three or more talking points relevant to the topic.
- Link talking points to pain points experienced by your buyers.
- Map your product/service value to the pain points (i.e., demonstrate how you solve the problem and do it better than your competition).
- Include a list of discovery questions and prompts the rep can use to further the conversation.

Email Templates

Email templates are similar to call outlines, but for a written rather than spoken pitch. As a general rule, emails should be succinct and relevant to the recipient. Keep in mind that the prevalence of remote work and the way we access information both mean that the recipient is very likely to view your message on their mobile device. Using bullet points and keeping it brief will increase the chances of your message being read. Avoid talking about your company and focus instead on the value to your audience.

When determining content, remember that the recipient will be asking themselves these questions:

- Why should I read this?
- Are you solving a problem for me?
- Is this worth my time?

Email message templates can be shared easily with your teams as a way to make them more efficient in their email correspondence. There are many tools available today to draft messages, share templates, and track responses, allowing you to make the most impactful email templates available to your entire team. This is also a great opportunity to leverage AI functionality where available to assist with scaling this effort. As with call outlines, the individual reps should be encouraged to edit the template and personalize it before reaching out to customers and buyers.

Common Use Cases

There are typically five to ten common use cases that your product or service supports. It's critical that the GTM team be able to easily recognize these use cases and map them to solutions that solve for the needs of your buyers.

To build out resources to support this, you'll want to partner with Product Marketing, Product, and tenured reps from Sales and Success to determine and document the top five to ten use cases. Once you have your top use case list, document the following information for each one:

- Pain points/opportunities
- Negative consequences of the pain for your customers
- How you solve them
- How you solve them better than your competitors
- Expected results from leveraging your product/services
- How the results can be measured by your customers
- Proof points from third-party validation

To take it a step further, also include discovery questions that the Sales and Success teams can use when having conversations with customers and buyers related to the relevant use cases. Doing so will help create urgency to move a deal along in the initial sales process or retain and expand existing customer usage. Include discovery questions for the following prompts:

- Pain points
- Negative consequences of pains
- Positive outcome possibilities
- Required capabilities (priority, timeline, stakeholders, tech stack)
- Metrics

Make the use cases easily accessible to your Sales and Success teams via your knowledge management system (KMS) or content management system (CMS). Review and update use cases at least once a year, when launching new products or entering new markets targeting new verticals, segments, or personas.

Success Stories or Case Studies

As the saying goes, facts tell, but stories sell. Third-party validation via success stories and case studies can be vital to closing and retaining customers. Stories help your customers and buyers envision how they can benefit from your solution, and they provide proof that your product/service is worth the investment. Customers and buyers are more likely to believe a customer that is similar to themselves over a rep who is paid to sell or service a product.

Your teams can never have enough stories. Stories can be archived/shared in the form of Marketing-produced case studies, but they can also be tribal knowledge stories from the front lines that are shared informally amongst the team. Tribal knowledge stories can come from sales reps, CSMs, SEs, PMs, and really anyone who speaks to your customers regularly. Your goal in Enablement is to curate as many stories as possible and make them readily available to your GTM teams via your KMS/CMS.

Note: Be sure to clearly designate how each story can be used and if there are any limitations that need to be taken into account. Examples of this are noting which stories can be used in writing with full information (these are usually the Marketing-sourced ones) vs. ones where you can share scenarios and outcomes based on an industry, use case, or business challenge, but you need to be careful not to mention company names.

Chapter 19 Debrief:
- What areas of selling do you think your customer-facing teams struggle with the most?
- Which of these selling challenges do you think could be addressed (at least partially) by having better resources available?
- Which resources do you think would be the most impactful? Why and how?

Applied Learning:
- Create an inventory of all your existing playbooks, messaging outlines (phone, voicemail, email), use cases, and case studies/customer stories.
    - Are these resources up to date, and are they still relevant to your current stage of growth, roles/team structures, products/services, and market positioning?
    - If not, would the update process (for each one) be a refresh or a complete overhaul?
- Use the results of your resource audit and your answers regarding which resources you think would be the most impactful to have a meeting with GTM leadership.
    - During this meeting, gather their thoughts on where they think the biggest challenges are and which corresponding resources they think would be most impactful.
    - Work with them to sketch out a priority list for any required refresh/update effort of resources.
- Based on your meeting with GTM leadership, their input, and the priorities list, create an initial plan and timeline to start updating priority resources.
    - As part of this plan, you need to determine which updates you can accomplish by yourself and how much involvement you will need from other SMEs (Marketing, Product, Sales, etc.).

Chapter 20:
Technology Systems and Tools

GTM Enablement often leads the effort or is a key stakeholder in procuring the systems and tools that the GTM team uses to be efficient and consistent in their customer interactions. Additionally, it is often the responsibility of the Enablement function to train the users on the systems and tools implemented for the GTM team.

Your needs will vary depending on the industry you are in, the size of your GTM team, the complexity of your sales/success process, etc. There are a lot of great technologies that can dramatically increase efficiency, consistency, and effectiveness, and they are definitely worth leveraging if you're clear about your needs and what you want technology to accomplish for your team.

The typical tech stack leveraged by a GTM team includes:
- CRM—Operations will typically chose these tools and partner with GTM Enablement to train the teams on how to best use them
- Email-tracking tools to share templates and track open, click-through, and response rates

- Prospecting tools to identify target buyers and their contact information
- Knowledge management and content management systems (KMS/CMS) for just-in-time trusted information and resources
- Project/stage and forecast management tools to track deal and account progress/activities—usually for larger deals and accounts when there are multiple stakeholders and long sales cycles
- Learning management system (LMS) to scale the Enablement function by delivering self-paced asynchronous learning modules, paths, and certifications and track completion and scores
- Call coaching software to record and provide scalable coaching on customer-facing calls
- Video call communication system for live virtual training events

Note of caution: It's common for tech companies to get "tech tool happy" and implement too many tools. The tools become redundant, which is not only costly, but also leads to system and tool fatigue on your teams. When people get overwhelmed and start opting out, cherry-picking which tools they want to use, creating manual workarounds, etc., inconsistency emerges quickly and best practices devolve.

To be effective, you must be strategic and purposeful in your technology choices. Select only the tools most appropriate to your needs, and train the teams to use them correctly—and then continue to support the tool. Going narrow but deep will prevent your team from getting stuck in "tool of the day" syndrome. On that note, it's a good idea to do a periodic tech stack audit to evaluate tool usage and determine which tools are being well utilized. Of course, if a tool is no longer serving your team (especially as you grow), you may be forced to evaluate whether you still need it and perhaps find a replacement if you need a better feature set, etc. Be very careful, though, to make these changes thoughtfully so as not to cause unnecessary havoc within the team.

Related *Fueling the Revenue Engine* Podcast Episode:
- Episode 3: What Should Be in Your Sales Enablement Tech Stack?

Chapter 20 Debrief:
- What GTM technologies have you used in the past that you liked? Why?
- Do you think your GTM teams are utilizing the specific tools within the tech stack well?
- Do you think your company is tech tool heavy, light, or just about right?

Applied Learning:
- Similar to the resource development section, create an inventory of your company's GTM tech stack.
  - Are these technologies being used, and are they still a good fit for your current stage of growth and roles/team structures?
  - If not, are there tools/tech that you should consider dropping or updating?
- Use your answers above regarding GTM tech stack usage and fit to meet with GTM leadership and assess the GTM tech stack.
  - During this meeting with leadership, gather their thoughts on what technologies they would like to keep, drop, or update.
  - For any technologies that need an update or change, determine the criteria for a new solution.
  - After the meeting, research potential options for new technologies.

Reference Guide: Resources and Glossary

Below please find our recommended resources for you to continue learning about the field of GTM enablement. Many of Level 213's onboarding guidelines, templates, and worksheets that were presented within the chapters of this book are available on our website: level213.com.

For additional support on any of these topics and more, you can reach us at level213.com/contact.

Suggested Resources

Podcast:
- Level213, *Fueling the Revenue Engine*, Podbean, 2020, level213.com/fueling-the-revenue-engine-podcast

Books:
- Blount, Jeb. Sales EQ: How Ultra High Performers Leverage Sales-Specific Emotional Intelligence to Close the Complex Deal. Wiley, 2017.
- Boser, Ulrich. Learn Better: Mastering the Skills for Success in Life, Business, and School; or, How to Become an Expert in Just About Anything. Rodale, 2017.
- Catmull, Ed. Creativity, Inc.: Overcoming the Unseen Forces That Stand in the Way of True Inspiration. Random House, 2023.
- Dirksen, Julie. *Design for How People Learn*. New Riders, 2016.
- Kahneman, Daniel. *Thinking Fast and Slow*. Farrar, Straus and Giroux, 2011.
- Kunkle, Mike. *The Building Blocks of Sales Enablement*. Association for Talent Development, 2021.

- Madian, T. Melissa. Enabler? I Hardly Know Her!: How to Make the Sales Experience Not Suck. Tellwell Talent, 2020.
- Matthews, Bryon, and Tamara Schenk. Sales Enablement: A Master Framework to Engage, Equip, and Empower a World-Class Sales Force. Wiley, 2018.
- Pink, Daniel. To Sell Is Human: The Surprising Truth About Moving Others. Riverhead Books, 2013.
- Roberge, Mark. The Sales Acceleration Formula: Using Data, Technology, and Inbound Selling to go from $0 to $100 Million. Wiley, 2015.
- Sisakhti, Reza. Success in Selling: Developing a World-Class Sales Ecosystem. ATD Press, 2016.

Organizations:

- Modern Sales Pros: modernsaleshq.com
- ATD Sales Enablement Group: td.org/topics/sales-enablement
- Revenue Enablement Society: sesociety.org
- Sales Enablement Pro: community.highspot.com
- The Enablement Squad: enablementsquad.com
- Sales Enablement Collective: salesenablementcollective.com

Glossary

Although we've defined many of these references within relevant sections, the list below presents common terms and acronyms commonly used by revenue teams and corporate organizations.

- Adult learning theory (andragogy): the practice of teaching and educating adults
- AE: Account executive
- AM: Account manager
- Asynchronous learning: self-paced learning, not in real time, often distributed via a learning management system (LMS)
- BDR: business development representative

- Bloom's Taxonomy: a hierarchical model designed by Benjamin Bloom, used to classify educational learning objectives into levels of complexity and specificity
- CMS: content management system
- CRM: customer relationship management (system)
- CSM: customer success manager
- EBR: executive business review
- FLM: front-line manager
- GA: general availability, i.e., the release of a product to the general public
- GTM: go-to-market
- KMS: knowledge management system
- KPI: key performance indicator
- LMS: learning management system
- MKO: midyear kickoff
- MLO: micro learning object
- MQL: marketing qualified lead
- MSA: master service(s) agreement
- OTE: on target earnings, which equals a rep's total compensation from base salary plus commission when they meet their quota
- PM: product manager, project manager, or program manager
- PMM: product marketing manager
- PR: product release
- QBR: quarterly business review
- ROE: rules of engagement
- ROI: return on investment
- SaaS: software as a service
- SDR: sales development representative
- SE: sales engineer or solutions engineer
- SKO: sales kickoff
- SME: subject matter expert
- SQL: sales qualified lead

Citations

Chapter 1

Level213, host. "Why, What and How of Enablement." Fueling the Revenue Engine, episode 1, Podbean, 21 May 2020. rozgre.podbean.com/e/why-what-and-how-of-enablement

Level213, host. "The Intersection of Revenue Operations and Enablement." Fueling the Revenue Engine, episode 17, Podbean, 8 April 2022. rozgre.podbean.com/e/the-intersection-of-revenue-operations-enablement

Level213, host. "Strong Sales Enablement and Product Marketing Partnerships." Fueling the Revenue Engine, episode 9, Podbean, 8 April 2022. rozgre.podbean.com/e/strong-sales-enablement-product-marketing-partnerships

Chapter 2

Bridge Group. Sales Development Report: Models, Metrics and Compensation Research. 2023. blog.bridgegroupinc.com/hubfs/resources/TBG%202023%20Sales%20Development%20Report.pdf

CSO Insights. Sales Enablement Optimization Study. 2016. cdn2.hubspot.net/hubfs/4460233/SocialSellinator-June2019/PDF/2016-Sales-Enablement-Optimization-Study.pdf

Level213, host. "True Partnership Between Sales Leadership and Enablement." Fueling the Revenue Engine, episode 2, Podbean, 27 May 2020. rozgre.podbean.com/e/true-partnership-between-sales-leadership-and-enablement

Madian, T. Melissa. "Get Your Sales Teams to Tell Stories Your Customers Care About." LinkedIn. 26 June 2015. linkedin.com/pulse/get-your-sales-teams-tell-stories-customers-care-t-melissa-madian

Sanghavi, Aayushi. "70+ Sales Enablement Statistics to Blow Your Mind in 2024." G2. 16 February 2024. learn.g2.com/sales-enablement-statistics

Ye, Leslie. "Sales-Marketing Alignment Increases Revenue by 208%." Hubspot Blog. 28 July 2017. blog.hubspot.com/sales/sales-marketing-alignment-increases-revenue-infographic

Chapter 4

Level213, host. "Metrics Driven Enablement." Fueling the Revenue Engine, episode 11, Podbean, 17 September 2020. rozgre.podbean.com/e/metrics-driven-enablement

Chapter 6

Level213, host. "Designing Training for Salespeople." Fueling the Revenue Engine, episode 6, Podbean, 24 June 2020, rozgre.podbean.com/e/designing-training-for-salespeople.

Chapter 7

Bloom, Benjamin S. Taxonomy of Educational Objectives: Handbook I: The Cognitive Domain. David McKay Company, Inc., 1956.

Chapter 10

Level213, host. "Agile Approaches to Sales Enablement." Fueling the Revenue Engine, episode 7, Podbean, 8 July 2020. rozgre.podbean.com/e/agile-approaches-to-sales-enablement

Zenger, Jack, J. Folkman, and R. Sherwin. "The Promise of Phase Three." Training and Development 59.1 (2005): 30–35.

Chapter 11

Level213, host. "Optimizing Onboarding in a Hybrid World." Fueling the Revenue Engine, episode 16, Podbean, 11 March 2022. rozgre.podbean.com/e/optimizing-onboarding-in-a-hybrid-world

Chapter 13

Leikam, Amanda. "Broken or Just Missing Some Pieces? Diagnosing Sales Process Shortcomings." Next Level Thoughts, 13 October 2017. level213.com/blog/2017/10/13/broken-or-just-missing-some-pieces-diagnosing-sales-process-shortcomings

Chapter 14

Level213, host. "Strong Sales Enablement & Product Marketing Partnerships." Fueling the Revenue Engine, episode 9, Podbean, 30 July 2020. rozgre.podbean.com/e/strong-sales-enablement-product-marketing-partnerships

Chapter 16

Level213, host. "In the Trenches: AE Perspective on Enablement." Fueling the Revenue Engine, episode 8, Podbean, 16 July 2020. rozgre.podbean.com/e/in-the-trenches-ae-perspective-on-enablement

Chapter 17

Level213, host. "Enablement Guide to Sales Coaching." Fueling the Revenue Engine, episode 18, Podbean, 29 April 2022. rozgre.podbean.com/e/enablement-guide-to-sales-coaching

Chapter 18

Level213, host. "Rethinking SKO in a Virtual World." Fueling the Revenue Engine, episode 12, Podbean, 15 October 2020. rozgre.podbean.com/e/rethinking-sko-in-a-virtual-world

Chapter 20

Level213, host. "What Should Be in Your Sales Enablement Tech Stack?" Fueling the Revenue Engine, episode 3, Podbean, 3 June 2020. rozgre.podbean.com/e/what-should-be-in-your-sales-enablement-tech-stack

Acknowledgments

This book has been decades in the making and truly represents the culmination of our professional endeavors with thousands of revenue professionals. In addition to the large, strategic, and enduring building blocks that have shaped our approach, there were also many powerful insights that emerged from quieter moments and seemingly routine conversations. What started out as intuition, trial and error, and pilot programs for teams of all sizes and phases of maturity has become our blueprint, best practice, and a standard of excellence for revenue enablement.

We would like to express deep gratitude for our clients, mentors, coaches, colleagues, managers, coworkers, direct reports, and technology partners whom we have had the privilege of working with over the past 25+ years. The daily challenges that are inherent to working with revenue teams often result in difficult conversations and decision points. We thank you for your part in the conversations that produced profound change and the lessons that shaped our own development.

A special thank you goes to our editing and graphics team. Brook Cosby, your meticulous attention to detail and continuous growth mindset challenged us to articulate our thoughts in meaningful ways that allow readers to build on foundational knowledge and then take action. Rusty Howson, your design expertise lies well beyond our abilities and brings a much needed visual element to our intellectual frameworks and prose.

And we can't conclude without acknowledging the grounding presence of our natural world and its ever present counterbalance to the technology-driven community we call GTM.

About the Authors

Roz Greenfield

After a successful career as a top producing sales rep and sales manager, Roz Greenfield spent 10+ years in revenue enablement for tech companies, developing and training superior sales and success teams. She successfully led sales enablement groups working with sales teams in both the large global enterprises and small to mid-size startup SaaS companies. Driven by her desire to have a larger impact and work with more organizations, Roz co-founded Level213, where she provides solutions for critical revenue and go-to-market enablement challenges.

When not working with revenue teams, Roz can be found guiding forest bathing walks for people who want to counteract the high velocity and stress of daily life by connecting with nature.

Amanda Leikam

Amanda Leikam brings more than 25 years of experience working with technology companies in sales, operations, management, coaching, and consulting roles. Amanda has worked with organizations of all sizes, ranging from early stage startups to global enterprises. As co-founder of Level213, Amanda excels at working with growing companies looking to level up their customer-facing revenue teams, with a focus on assessments, sales process, training and resource development, learning integration, sales coaching, leadership development, and executive coaching.

High-performance sports have been a central theme of Amanda's life. As a teenager, she raced for the US National Cycling Team and trained at the US Olympic Training Center. Amanda also holds a black belt in Tae Kwon Do and competed on the US Equestrian Federation jumper circuit.

www.ingramcontent.com/pod-product-compliance
Lightning Source LLC
Chambersburg PA
CBHW071459220526
45472CB00003B/854